EVERYDAY LEGACY

EVERYDAY LEGACY

LESSONS FOR LIVING WITH PURPOSE, RIGHT NOW

CODI SHEWAN

PAGE TWO BOOKS

Cataloguing in publication information is available from
Library and Archives Canada.
ISBN 978-1-989025-99-4 (paperback)
ISBN 978-1-989603-00-0 (ebook)

Page Two
www.pagetwo.com

Cover design by Peter Cocking and Jennifer Lum
Cover image by H. Armstrong Roberts/ClassicStock,
via Getty Images
Interior design by Jennifer Lum and Peter Cocking
Printed and bound in Canada by Friesens
Distributed in Canada by Raincoast Books
Distributed in the US and internationally by
Publishers Group West, a division of Ingram

20 21 22 23 24   5 4 3 2 1

www.everydaylegacy.com

Some names and identifying details have been changed
to protect the privacy of individuals.

For Eric and my family, whose love shapes my human experience in such powerful ways. I love you all, so much. This book is for you.

CONTENTS

INTRODUCTION

THE STORY OF OUR LIVES

SPENT TWENTY years working as a funeral director and embalmer. While I long ago lost track of the number of funerals I've arranged and directed, I can remember so many of the people I assisted and, among the strife of those I cared for, tender moments that still echo today.

Two funerals in particular changed me forever. The first was the funeral of a man named Bob, my estranged father, who taught me more after his death than he did while he was alive. You'll read about this experience later in this book.

The second funeral that changed my outlook took place a few years into my career. I was listening to the service through the speakers at the back of the chapel, as I always did. One thing I loved about my job was learning about the lives people led before coming into my care. As always, the guest of honor lay in a casket at the front of the room while his loved ones took turns sharing stories about him. Something about the way they described him—generous, kind, always there to lend a hand, loyal, loving—stirred me.

Along with their stories came a gamut of emotions. At some points people sobbed, while at others they were laughing. Tears of sadness mixed with those from belly laughs. It was such a joyful celebration of this individual's life. I had seen other, similar funerals, but for some reason, at this one, I recall thinking, *I sure hope this man knows the influence he had on these people.*

Did he know what he meant to the people in that room?

Did he live every day with the awareness that he meant so much to so many?

Did he live that way on purpose?

Then a notion hit me and my mind began to spin. I'd always associated "legacy" with the end and thought of it as something we leave behind. In an instant, I resolved that I didn't want just to leave my legacy behind when I died. I wanted to live my legacy, every day. To live consciously and cultivate an ever-present awareness of the impact I have on the people in my life.

If I lived the way I wanted to be remembered, how would that change me and those around me?

At that moment, I vowed to always strive to live my legacy every single day. And part of my legacy, I decided, would be to inspire others to do the same.

I recently attended a gala event for an association, and a woman with whom I had been at a mastermind retreat several months earlier was seated beside me. Evelynn and I hadn't known each other well when we met at the retreat, but after spending three solid days together, we'd shared a fair bit about ourselves. We happened to be partnered for an exercise during which we were asked to share what was most important to us at the time, and I told her about *Everyday Legacy*. I was nearly done writing it, and I said that I was about to begin editing and considering my publishing options. She asked me to tell her more about the book—not about the logistics of writing it, but about its philosophy. So I did. And as I explained one of the concepts, her eyes brimmed with tears, a physical signal that the message I was conveying resonated with her on a deep, personal level. She said that, as I spoke, she was thinking about her relationships. When I finished, she cupped my hand in hers and thanked me for sharing. The next day, we went our separate ways.

Now here we were months later, seated beside each other. When the meal was finished, she leaned toward me and, over the music, said, "I'd like to tell you something."

We shifted our chairs closer together, and I moved in to listen.

"I'm so thankful we met at that retreat. I really enjoyed speaking with you."

I agreed with her. Our meeting was a highlight of the mastermind for me, too.

She squeezed my hand and looked at me with an intensity that commanded attention. "You don't understand," she said. "Your sharing about *Everyday Legacy* with me has changed the way I live my life."

I sat, speechless, thinking, *My book? Has changed how she lives?*

While my mind raced, overwhelmed, all I could do was look back at her and say, "Thank you." I was honored and flattered and, quite honestly, taken aback. Then a thought entered my mind.

I did it.

She said, "So when do you publish? When is the rest of the world going to hear your message?"

I smiled and replied, "Now, after hearing what you just shared, it doesn't matter."

She looked at me quizzically and said, "I'm confused. What do you mean?"

"When I wrote my book, my goal was to impact one person. While I wrote it, I realized I was already doing that. It was influencing me, and that was enough. Now I realize I've affected one more person."

She smiled back. "Everyone needs this message," she said. "It will help people live more consciously and with greater purpose, and the world needs that right now."

At that moment, I felt such humility. At the time of our conversation, I'd been feeling particularly vulnerable about releasing this—my first book—into the world. She had no idea how profoundly her words affected me and that they were exactly what I needed to hear, at exactly the right time.

It may come as a surprise to some, but a career spent staring death in the face every day hasn't taught me anything about dying. It has, however, taught me everything I know about living. This book comprises stories from my life and the lessons I've learned from living my own Everyday Legacy. My hope is that you will see yourself in these stories or recognize the situations, or you may relate to the lessons on some level.

Storytelling has been used as a tool to pass on lessons and to teach one another for as long as there have been human beings. *Everyday Legacy* is about drawing on experience through story and finding the relatable context that steers you more powerfully and purposefully toward your true self. It's about helping you to live the characteristics and values that are important to you, so that you're proud of what you're giving the world while you're still alive.

This is not a step-by-step "how-to" guide. It's a book meant to inspire conversations between you and yourself, first and foremost, to encourage you to live the way you want to be remembered after death. Every person is unique, as are your stories, your values, and your virtues. Whoever you are and whatever your story, this book will change everything you think you know about legacy. Forever. And maybe, just maybe, as happened with Evelynn, it might change your life.

1

THE
STICKER
BOOK

FINDING CONNECTION

LOVED COLLECTING stickers when I was a kid. My mother would give me colored stars when I completed my chores, as did my teachers when I completed my schoolwork. Just like most of the kids at school, I collected any sticker I could get my hands on, and I managed to accumulate quite a few.

I needed a place to keep all these treasures, but my family didn't spend money unnecessarily. They were frugal and, for the most part, bought only things we needed, so a sticker book was *not* going to find its way into the budget. My mother, tired of me bugging her for one, gave me an old photo album to use instead. It had a shimmery green cover and gold coil binding. It was the kind of album with sticky pages where you sandwich the photo between the adhesive and the sheet of acetate plastic. It turned out to be perfect for stickers.

That sticker book became one of my favorite things, and I carried it around the house with me constantly. I often flipped through it, admiring my collection.

When I was about seven years old, tragedy struck my small town when a young hockey player died in a car crash. I recall seeing the story about his death in the newspaper. I liked playing hockey, and so I somehow identified with him.

That was the first time I'd heard of a young person, not an old man or woman, passing away. I kept looking at the photo that accompanied the article. It showed the pallbearers carrying his small casket. They weren't much older than me. I felt so curious about this boy. He died, but who was he? What did he like to do with his friends? What was his favorite hobby?

I was so interested that I cut the entire story out of the paper and carefully folded it up, like origami, so only the photo was showing. I placed it on top of the acetate on one of the pages of my sticker book, using four stickers to hold down the corners of the picture, as if giving it a frame.

In the small community where I grew up, everyone had the opportunity to publish an obituary, free of charge, in the local newspaper. This wasn't a death notice with the sole intention of notifying the community that someone had died and stating the details of the visitation and funeral. These obituaries were often printed about a month after a person had passed away. They were stories, usually accompanied by photographs. These obituaries talked about who the people were and where they had been born; what they loved to do in their spare time; their philanthropic endeavors; their familial connections; their passions. A column or two became space that enveloped a lifetime.

After the death of the young hockey player, something inexplicably attracted me to reading these obituaries. In my mind's eye, I brought the people back to life, visualizing them living out the scenarios described in the columns. I started snipping obituaries from the newspaper and adding them to my sticker book, to go with the story about the hockey player. Not all of them—just the ones I found interesting. The ones that most vividly came to life when I imagined them.

I lived in a rural area, and there weren't many other people my age to play with. I didn't have many friends. To me, those people in my sticker book became a cast of characters. Their stories helped me to feel a deeper human connection that, as a young boy, I didn't realize I craved.

This behavior lasted until just before I became a teenager.

The human condition has always interested me, and this is true now more than ever. How and why do people come into each other's lives when they do? Why do they have a significant influence, or none at all? I'm fascinated by the value that relationships either do or don't bring. Why do some people enter our lives and why do others leave? Why do some people have such a commanding role while others recede?

Love and relationships come in all different shapes and sizes and dimensions. Growing up in a rural place, all I had was home and school. Community, as many people know it, didn't play a large role in my life. We didn't have a neighborhood, per se. My family home was in a remote location. Up the road we had a "neighbor," whose house we could barely see from the end of our driveway. The people in my sticker book became friends I could look forward to meeting when the paper landed in our mailbox every day. These friends came to me; I didn't have to go looking for them. Sometimes one arrived, sometimes two, sometimes eight at a time.

I read the pieces about them and learned how these people lived. I saw who they were connected to and what mattered to them. I had a view of who they were and how they showed up in the world. At the time, I had no concept of legacy; I was a kid. These were just people who had been born and then they died. I wanted to know what happened in between. If I found them interesting, they made the cut. Literally. Into my sticker book.

My fascination with obituaries marked the beginning of something that has gone on to define my life: my quest for human story—human connection and relationships.

I wish I could reach through these pages and learn more about you. I hope that, after you finish reading this book, you will reach out and connect with me. But first, I need to tell you more about what Everyday Legacy is all about.

So let's fast-forward, to the next page, to the end of your life.

2

LIVING YOUR EVERYDAY LEGACY

LEAVING THE WORLD BETTER

YOU'RE DEAD. Your human experience is over. I'm going to give you the opportunity to talk to the person who meant the most to you. But the only question you're allowed to ask is, "What will I be remembered for?" What do you think you'll hear?

That you were honest? Loyal? That you always had something positive to say? That you brought comfort to any situation? That you made people laugh? That you made everyone around you smile and feel alive?

Or might that person struggle to tell you how you're being remembered?

Did you put your job above most things? Or, worse, did you put work above everything? Did money matter more than the things that money can't buy? Did you take time for people when they needed you? Or did you only make time when it was convenient for you?

The first thing being a funeral director taught me was that death has no clock; it waits for no one. Death can be as close as the next minute. When it's your time, it's your time. But you get to determine how you live before that time comes.

I am willing to bet that, when you hear the name Nobel, you instantly think of the Nobel Peace Prize. But perhaps you aren't aware that this association exists because Alfred Nobel had the unusual opportunity to read his own obituary, and he did not like what had been written.

Alfred Nobel invented dynamite. He made a fortune by stabilizing TNT so it would be safer to work with and to transport. Essentially, Alfred Nobel armed the world with bombs.

When his brother Ludvig Nobel died, a French newspaper mistakenly printed a scathing obituary for Alfred. The piece reported on the passing of the "merchant of death" who grew rich by inventing new ways to "mutilate and kill." It is believed that when Alfred read this, he became obsessed with the way he would be remembered after his death.

And so, Alfred Nobel rewrote his last will and testament, arranging that his fortune would be used to recognize and award peace. He wanted to be remembered for his philanthropy, not as someone whose life's work took the lives of so many.

Had he not read those harsh words, the world would have a very different memory of him.

Although historians have never found this obituary, and even if this story of Alfred Nobel is a modern myth, it teaches a powerful lesson about how we should live.

Often, when we talk about learning lessons, we don't necessarily imply that the lesson learned will result in actual changes in behavior. But when we read stories like Alfred Nobel's, whether they are historically accurate or not, they offer us something to apply in our lives.

Lessons lived are much different from lessons learned. A lesson lived means understanding what you've been taught, adopting it, and executing it with action. Lessons learned mean nothing unless they're applied.

You have to live the lessons you learn.

In one of my workshops, I conduct an exercise that involves people writing their own obituaries. This is a powerful practice because it forces you to consider the end and to think about what's important and how you want to be remembered.

What if you thought now about the things and the people in your life, taking note of everything that you value. If you were to fast-forward to the end, which of the things would become irrelevant?

What's left when you strip away the things that don't really matter?

What's left is people. Not things. Not possessions. Not bank accounts. At least not for most of us.

Think about the people in your life and what you mean to them. What is it about you that they love? What values and qualities do you possess that they hold dear?

People's opinions of us are a manifestation of our behavior. If you have likable characteristics, you will be well liked. If you don't conduct yourself nicely, you're not going to be very well thought of.

Since outside opinions of us correlate to our behavior, we have to decide: who do we show up as in this world?

Who do you show up as?

The way you behave today will be the way you are remembered tomorrow.

DEATH IS NOT ON A CLOCK

Death is not on a clock. When you're consciously aware of that fact, and it drives you forward to live the values you want to be remembered for, that's Everyday Legacy. The end is quite possibly as close to you as it is far away. Most of us aren't afforded the luxury of knowing how near or how far the end is.

This awareness has the power to drive your behavior. It reminds you to say, "I love you." To have deep conversations. To never go to bed angry. To never part ways with a loved one with any negativity occupying space in the relationship. To choose your words carefully, because one day what you say will be your last words to that person. Perhaps your last words at all.

This awareness teaches us to be more gracious.

Picture this: A man jumps ahead of a woman in a line for coffee, because he's on his way to an important interview, only to find out the interviewer was the person he cut ahead of. How do you think that works out for him?

We never know the power of a moment. We never know the power of a gesture.

Walking through life with this awareness gives us more profound clarity about who we are, who we show up as, and how we affect the world. Whether one person or every person we meet is touched by our kindness, one person is better than no one, and kind acts always have a ripple effect.

In a world where individuals feel as though they have very little control over anything, you are in control of how you behave, on every level, in every interaction, including with yourself.

Let's think back to the story of Alfred Nobel. If, as he did, you could hear what's said about you after you die, would you like what you hear?

Would you be surprised by who showed up at your funeral, or hurt by who didn't? Would you be happy with what was said, or disappointed about what was left unacknowledged?

Would imagining how you'll be remembered cause you to shift every day of your life?

By living with mindfulness, we can control how we'll be remembered. I want to be known as making a difference in people's lives. Making them laugh, giving incredible hugs, making people know I love them. For me, that sums up influence. I want to affect how people feel, in a positive way.

When you're dead on an embalming table, all that's left is a shell, the physical vessel that carried you through life. Ultimately, all we leave behind are the feelings, the emotions, and the love, the memories that have the power to keep us alive in the hearts and minds of those we touched.

If you ask yourself, "If tomorrow were my last day, what would I be remembered for?" and you don't like what you hear, change your behavior. Live the way you want to be remembered so you can leave the world without regret.

It might sound like this will require a lot of work. But, as with anything you do that is of any magnitude, you just have to start.

START WITH ONE BRICK

The buildings with the most beautiful architecture in the world all started with one brick. The small church on the country road started with one brick, too.

Asking yourself that question—"What will I be remembered for?"—is laying that first brick; it starts the process of living your legacy. That question leads to deeper, more purposeful and powerful conversations with yourself and people who mean something to you, to dictate how you show up, to navigate toward your Everyday Legacy.

I would say that it's never too late to start living this way, but that would be a lie. Once you're gone, it's too late.

So, how do you want to be remembered? Take a moment to think about it.

If you're like most people, instinctively you may say something like, "I want to be remembered as a good mother/father/friend/teacher/nurse."

But that's not a legacy. Legacy isn't a title. Legacy isn't an occupation. It's who you are and it's what you give to people.

Saying something like, "I want to be remembered as an incredible parent," is a great starting point, but you have to break that down. What does it mean to be an incredible mother or father? You have to be patient and kind. Loving, attentive, and thoughtful. What are the tangible characteristics of being a good parent that you can sow into your daily life so that, over time, you'll be more than simply an incredible parent? Your patience and thoughtfulness will touch your children *and* every other person in your life.

To say that you want to be remembered as a wonderful teacher is a noble thing, but what does it mean?

To be a wonderful teacher, you must again be patient, but you also need to be inspiring and selfless with your time, to be there for children who might not have another great support person in their life. You must be empathetic and compassionate. Those qualities will light up the lives of your students, and they will be felt by others you meet, as well.

LIVING A LEGACY

A legacy is not like a will. It's not about bequeathing your assets to someone once you're gone, or distributing your wealth. Everyday Legacy is living purposefully while you're alive, in a way that uplifts the lives of others. It's about living the way you want to be remembered. That's it.

While I was writing this book, I started digging for stories about people who lived their legacies. I came across many quotes about leaving a legacy, but nothing about living a legacy. However, when I talk about *Everyday Legacy*, people tell me stories about people they know who lived their legacies. Like the woman who messaged me after she heard me deliver a keynote, to tell me about a loved one who passed away. She wrote: "Her death was sudden and tragic, but the mood in the room wasn't devastation and agony—it was gratitude. Joy, even. People were so grateful for her presence in their lives, her contribution to family and her joie de vivre. Truly someone who lived her legacy."

You can probably name people who lived or are living their legacies, whether they did or do so intentionally or not. One person who comes to mind for me is Malala Yousafzai.

When Malala was only eleven years old, she was blogging for the BBC about the Taliban attacking schools and their attempts to stop girls from becoming educated. Even though she used a pseudonym, her identity was eventually revealed.

Malala continued to speak out about her right, and the rights of all women, to be educated. While she and her family were concerned about their safety, they didn't believe the Taliban would attempt to kill a child. They were wrong.

At the age of fifteen, when she was riding a bus home from school, Malala was shot in the head.

But the bullet did not kill her. Nor did it kill her spirit. Instead of letting the Taliban weaken her resolve to pursue an education, the attack made her stronger.

On her sixteenth birthday, only nine months after she was shot, Malala gave a speech at the United Nations about education and women's rights. She strongly urged leaders of the world to change their policies. In addressing the assembly, she said, "Dear friends, on the 9th of October, 2012, the Taliban shot me on the left side of my forehead. They shot my friends, too. They thought that the bullets would silence us, but they failed. And out of that silence came thousands of voices."

At seventeen years old, Malala became the youngest person ever to receive the Nobel Peace Prize.

I don't know if Malala is living her Everyday Legacy consciously, but without a doubt she is aware of the change she's created in the world, and that awareness has helped her to magnify her impact.

There is something that Malala and you and I share. A common thread that connects us all. An absolute truth that is unquestionable.

Every one of us will die.

Just like the people in the newspaper that arrived in my family's mailbox daily. You and I may have completely different backgrounds, completely different socioeconomic statuses, be different races, genders, and ages. But one day we will all appear on the same page in the newspaper.

You are going to die. Creating an Everyday Legacy is about taking that inevitable fact and shifting your intention from leaving a legacy to living it. A great power exists in consciously living your legacy, every single day. Someone once said that while we will all die, not all of us live. Living a legacy is about embracing who we are and the gifts we can give to the world, and offering those qualities in our daily interactions, to shape how we live.

The beautiful part of this shift is that it makes the end irrelevant. Death could be anywhere on the horizon, but if you're living more purposefully and powerfully today, it doesn't matter where that end is.

This changes our relationship with death. Learning to live in a meaningful way quiets the fear of death because the resonance of our purpose is so loud.

Another aspect of living your Everyday Legacy is helping people become aware of what they will be remembered for. Once you're dialed into this energy, you'll naturally want to point out to others their unique greatness. So many people come and go from this life without ever understanding the real depth of the impact they had while they were here. Sadly, we often wait until someone has left this world before we verbalize what they, on a deeper level, meant to us. When you're living your legacy, you readily celebrate people while they're here, even in the smallest of ways, by telling them what they're doing that positively affects your life.

Think about that person who makes you laugh, who makes you feel lighter and brighter just by being around them. What if, as a child, they were programmed to believe that there's negativity around being funny? They may have been told to be more focused and to take things more seriously. That they shouldn't always be joking around.

What if you told that person that your mood always improves when you're around them? That the world is a better place with them in it, because they always make people laugh?

When you tell people the value they bring to us, instantly the things they're programmed to believe become less important. Not only that, but with new positive energy around these qualities, people start to lean closer to their truths.

How differently would someone behave if you told them, "I value your authenticity. When I speak with you, I know you are listening with purpose and that what you share with me is coming from a deep place of truth. I value that. It's so refreshing. Thank you."

Do you think saying this would make that person even more authentic during their next interaction? Of course it would! It aligns them more with their truth, and most likely they will behave this way even more often.

Pointing out others' gifts can create a shift, taking people from thinking they have little influence in the lives of others to manifesting their own legacies in more purposeful, scalable, significant, and powerful ways.

You may be thinking, *I do this! I am authentic! I'm on the right track!*

And you are, as long as your behavior is consistent. If you're behaving authentically now and again, here and there, that's not living your legacy on purpose. It's not active enough. If you wish to make authenticity your Everyday Legacy, you have to practice it *every day*, until it is as much a part of you as your eye color. And just like your eye color, your legacy will become something that people experience just by being in your presence.

YOUR TRUTH

Malala shows us that we don't have to come from riches or a lofty status to make a big difference. All we have to do is live our truth. And the more we lean into our truth, the more we experience the value of showing up with truth, honesty, and authenticity. We can change the world, one person at a time.

This happens when there's a conscious awareness around wanting to leave this world better than you found it. And the world starts with one person, who could be the person in the mirror staring back at you. Beyond yourself, you'll show people by example that touching one person makes a difference; and others soon realize that there's a common ingredient to living a legacy: Truth. Sometimes this truth is described with words like "impact" and "purpose" and "honesty." What propels people to show up the way they do, to create change in the world? It's their truth.

When we talk about changing the world, it sounds like a big place. And, physically, it is. But it's also small, especially when you think about the ripple effect that comes from your interactions with others. Changing the world happens through the ways you relate, every day. From this perspective, the person you live with is the world. The people in your family, they are the world. Maybe your community is the world, or maybe your country is.

You, me, Malala, we all have the ability to construct a building one brick at a time. We might have different-sized structures, but the important thing is just to lay that first brick.

3

WHERE
LESSONS LIVE

THE POWER OF LISTENING

NITIALLY, MY interest in the funeral business stemmed from a desire to become as affluent as my town's funeral director, who happened to be a family friend. We lived in a small town—a one-stop-sign-that-no-one-ever-stopped-at kind of small town. And everyone, for the most part, lived quite modestly. But the funeral director had everything my young mind could imagine wanting: a beautiful car, a gorgeous waterfront home, a boat, horses. I equated his career with the life I thought I wanted to have as an adult.

I pursued a career in funerals because I was after affluence. But, believe me, that attitude did not last for long.

I know now that I was purposely pulled toward the funeral-service profession. When asked, many funeral directors will say that they don't know what brought them to the business. In my experience, it felt like a calling. Something bigger than me was pushing me into that role.

To me, funeral directors are similar to firefighters, who run into the burning building when everyone else is doing the opposite. When everyone else runs away from death, funeral directors step up. They walk alongside numb, grief-stricken people. They spiritually and sometimes physically put their arms around the grieving and partner with them in the immediate days of their loss. Funeral directors gently encourage hope and stay present in times when most people want to flee and hide.

By leading with their hearts, funeral directors have the capacity to manage through those emotions and serve people in powerful, meaningful ways. So, although the money first attracted me to the business, something more significant kept me there.

During high school, when it came time to choose a co-op work placement, I immediately thought about the local funeral home. Because our families were friends, I was able to speak with the funeral director about arranging my work placement with him. He agreed, but with a condition: If I was going to work in the funeral profession, he wanted me to know what happened to people before they entered the funeral home's care. I should understand that the deceased had lives and stories and family members, who were often shattered, experiencing terrible grief. I had to know what that all looked like so I could be empathetic and see things from the perspective of those left behind. This early conversation with the funeral director hinted that there was far more to this career than affluence, after all.

I took his advice and split my co-op placement. I would begin working in the local hospital's palliative care unit. Then I would go to the funeral home. I was determined to succeed in my chosen career and, without fully understanding why, I was willing to do what this prosperous, generous man advised me to do. It turns out that he gave me some of the best advice I've ever received.

When I first arrived at the palliative care unit, the staff didn't know what to do with me. I was a seventeen-year-old kid. The candy stripers on duty already delivered books and treats to the patients. And I obviously couldn't provide any nursing care. So, I figured, the patients had books and candy, the least I could do was eat candy with them and read books to them. That's what I thought *before* I realized how sick the patients were. Looking back, I didn't fully understand what palliative care meant, but I learned pretty quickly.

Palliative care is where people go to die.

When people enter palliative care, their illness has progressed beyond treatment. There is no curative medicine to fix their condition, and the only type of care left is simply that. Care. Soothing care.

In most instances, I introduced myself to the patients, offered to read to them, and they would either take me up on my offer or they wouldn't. In the cases where I sat and read, I did so until they fell asleep. Or, if a visitor arrived, I would dog-ear my page, return the book to the bedside table, and excuse myself. With most patients, besides my reading and their listening, we didn't really interact. But there was one exception: Roy Brant.

In my seventeen-year-old perception, Roy didn't look or behave like the other patients. An Evangelical pastor, Roy was in his eighties and battling cancer. He was alert, lucid, chipper, spry, and curious. I thought perhaps they had run out of beds on other floors and this was the only spot for him.

Roy and I sat and talked together, always having great conversations. But without uttering a single word, he filled the room with his genuineness. When he did speak, you knew he had a depth of character that deserved your attention. Although there was a very wide gap in our ages, Roy had stories to share and a heart that needed to be listened to, and I was a kid with the same needs. I couldn't believe I was getting high school credits for learning the wisdom of days gone by.

Roy was curious about why such a young man was volunteering his time in palliative care—a place where people went to meet their Maker. He asked me why I chose to be there, of all places, and when I shared my reasons, he was intrigued by my fascination with the funeral profession. A pastor by profession, Roy had performed hundreds of funerals for his parishioners over the years, and here I was, a young man so interested in the lives of those who had died.

Every day, I looked forward to seeing Roy. He needed someone to help him pass the time, and I was that person. I didn't consider the value I was gaining through this arrangement. I wasn't looking for anything from our relationship. But I had made a choice to show up, without realizing the effects that simply sitting together—sharing what was on our hearts and minds, and paying attention to what was on the heart and mind of the other—might have on both of us.

During the two months I worked in the palliative unit, I met Roy's wife and his daughter. Whenever his wife arrived, I would politely excuse myself, but she would often insist that I stay. Roy had spent his life on the pulpit, conveying what he believed to be the truth through his words. I was another person for him to pass wisdom on to—and I was listening. His wife could see the sense of purpose he drew from our time together.

Roy was never preachy with me. He was just a grandfatherly-type figure who understood that he might have a meaningful influence on my life. And he did. Not only because of the stories he told me but because he heard my words, too. He didn't dismiss me or my thoughts because I was young, which some older people might. He took my opinions and ideas to heart.

Roy knew what he believed. He was generous with his love and wisdom, and I loved him. He once wrote a poem for me. Printed on the page was a photo of himself in the top left corner and one of me on the right. His wife had it printed and framed for me. The poem speaks of how two different generations could share so much with each other, if everyone took the time to realize this.

My time in the palliative care unit came to an end, but one day during my placement at the funeral home, I returned to the hospital for a casual visit. I followed the steps I had taken many times before, exiting the elevator and turning right, instinctually going to check on Roy first. Throughout my placement, I had always seen him first, said hello, and told him I would be back to stay longer, later. Of all the patients on the palliative care floor, none had the gravitational pull of Roy.

Looking forward to catching up, I walked down the hall to his door, but when I peeked inside, my heart fell. There was a perfectly made bed in an empty room.

I knew what a made bed and an empty room meant. I had seen it many times before. It indicated the person had died.

Hurrying to the nurses' station to see what had happened, I was relieved to hear that Roy had not died. Surprisingly, his cancer had become more manageable. I was so beyond grateful that he was alive and no longer had to be in the hospital. He had returned home to the care of his wife.

Roy hung on to life for a while longer. I was in my first year of college when he passed away. My mother and Roy's wife became close friends because of our connection. I was asked to be a pallbearer at Roy's funeral—the only non-family member to be given the honor.

In retrospect, the wisdom of many years allows me to say that, during my time volunteering at the hospital, I obviously needed to be with Roy. But back then, I spent all those hours with him because being with Roy was my favorite way to pass the time. I had a duty to complete a specified number of hours, and spending that time with Roy was meaningful for me.

In the end, all we have are memories. And for me, of all the things I learned in palliative care, the most important lessons came from listening.

It's through listening to stories and insights and wisdom and perspective that I figured out who Roy was and what was important to him, without him ever having to declare those things square on. I knew what his family meant to him. I knew what his wife meant to him. I knew what his church meant to him. I knew what I meant to him. It didn't take much for me to realize that the Roy I visited was tired and fighting a battle. And yet, often depleted, Roy still showed up with such presence and power that it was easy for me to imagine the force he must have been when he was well and full of energy.

Roy is a rare exception. The truth is that nothing survives palliative care—nothing, except the lessons. What we learn from listening just might live on forever.

4

MEETING BOB

UNCOVERING WHAT MATTERS

BOB AND I had a fractured relationship. He and my mother didn't stay together very long after I was born. They separated when I was about three years old. He was a gregarious man with a big personality. People liked him a lot. But he didn't turn out to be much of a husband. Or much of a father. I don't think he was a particularly good son, either.

After my parents separated, I saw very little of Bob. He and I were estranged, but connected through his mother. Feeling the burden of his apparent lack of interest in me, or lack of preparedness, or whatever distanced him from me, my grandmother tried to fill the void, and lovingly overcompensated.

My grandmother would give me things and say, "Your dad dropped this off for you. He wanted you to know he was thinking of you." At Christmastime, there were always presents under her tree for me. She would buy gifts and sign them, *Love, Dad.* She wanted me to feel loved by and connected to my father.

As a young boy, I was naive and hopeful; I wished things were better in the present and hoped they would improve, while at the same time I didn't believe they would change. My father's absenteeism from my life became a gaping chasm that grew and grew, to the point that it was so deep and wide, nothing could hide it.

When I was about seven years old, my mother remarried. I cried about it, and not because I was happy. She was marrying a man whom she loved but I didn't. I have grown to love and understand him, but at the time, he seemed like someone from another world.

Having grown up in a big family on a farm, he was a real "man's man." He was a laborer. He could fix cars and perform oil changes and cut firewood. I didn't know about such things. He was a different man from the kind I would become. Even as a boy, I knew that.

When stepparents come into your life, a common line is "I'm not here to replace your mother/father." But for me, there was nobody to replace. My mother's new husband had a role to play in my life, but I didn't know what having a father was like.

So, here we were. My mother married a man who would act as a fatherly placeholder in my life, while all the time my living, breathing father resided a mere fifteen miles away and seemingly didn't care about me much at all. It was a very confusing time.

The older I got, the more distant Bob became. When I was a teenager, he moved about an hour away from my mother and me. My grandmother still put the gifts under her tree, but I had learned to recognize her handwriting, and I stopped believing they were from him. My hope faded, and his true colors started to shine.

Every year at Christmas, I was obliged to visit him at his apartment, where he would smoke cigarettes, play darts, drink beer, and listen to 70s music. He was present, but he had no presence. He would give me a piece of art that he'd made. Not something that a kid looks forward to receiving, but he didn't have any money.

During each of those obligatory visits, while Bob smoked and watched TV, I curled up and slept. Once, as a young teenager, when my mother came to pick me up, I overheard an argument between her and Bob. He said, "All he does is come here and sleep. He's a lazy teenager."

Mom immediately came to my defense. "He is not at all like that. It is only when he's here," she said. "You have to make him feel welcome. Make him feel like you want him to be here."

Bob said, "He knows my door is always open."

"Bob, he is not your friend, he is your son. It isn't about having an open-door policy with your children. It's about meeting them where they need to be met, not the other way around."

Overhearing this conflict between my parents offered me a moment of clarity: Bob didn't want to exert the effort to be a father. That was the last time I stayed with him.

From then on, if I was driving in town and passed him walking down the street, I wouldn't wave. We were like living ghosts to one another. He was there, but he wasn't. I was there, but I wasn't.

The years ticked on and I went to college. I graduated. I lived in a different city. In my early twenties, my grandmother became afflicted with dementia, which broke my heart. She moved from her apartment to a retirement community and eventually to a nursing facility. But through all that, I didn't directly cross paths with Bob.

I went through school for mortuary science and became a funeral director and embalmer. I recall sometimes thinking, *Does my father expect me to help with his funeral when he dies? I hope not. Why would he even have a funeral? Funerals are to celebrate life, and I have nothing to celebrate about this man. Funerals matter to people when people matter to people. He doesn't matter to me.*

And then, on a random day, out of the blue, I got a phone call from my mother. "Codi, I don't know how you're going to take this, but Bob has died."

A wave of emotion passed through me, and I was mentally overwhelmed in an instant.

Emotions hit me that I didn't expect.

I had thought that, when the day finally came, he would die and my life would go on. The end. But my mother's news was utterly arresting, as was the entire experience surrounding his death. The idea that I didn't care had been all talk, and now I had to step up, execute certain decisions, and take care of things.

Meanwhile, that hope from my childhood, which I thought had long ago escaped me, suddenly resurfaced. Except that the possibility that things between me and Bob would improve had vanished.

It's over.

There's no righting this now, if it had been meant to be. It's done.

I felt lost. I didn't know what to think or do. I hadn't spoken to Bob in years. But here I was, his closest next of kin. My grandmother was in a nursing home, and we were losing more of her every day. Telling her was going to be difficult because she was his mother. She knew he was never going to be the father she hoped he might be, but he was still her son.

It was a surreal experience to make funeral arrangements, without any idea of his wishes, for a man I didn't know. Did he want to be cremated or buried? Where was the best place to start? How do you navigate in a space where you know so little?

Bob had one brother, my uncle, who after university had moved out west and stayed there. Bob and my uncle didn't have much of a relationship to begin with, and they'd spent their adult lives apart. All that my uncle and my father had in common were a last name and their familial connection. My uncle was very successful in business, and my father could barely keep a job. My uncle had shown me more fatherly concern in our short bursts of time together than his brother displayed to me in my entire life. Even though he and his brother had been virtual strangers, my uncle flew out to help me.

Funeral director Codi kicked in and handled logistics. I knew how to plan a service, write obituary notices; all those things that need to be done, I took care of. But when it came to other things I encouraged families to do—to celebrate a life and memorialize someone's values and who they were—those seemed impossible. Because I didn't know who he was. I knew only who he was not.

And that was not something I thought appropriate to celebrate.

We also had an apartment to clean out.

My uncle and I had never been to Bob's place before.

Entering it was like walking through the door of a stranger's apartment. The smell of cigarette smoke clung to every surface. He was an artist, so he had a studio area where he kept paints and brushes. There was a TV with some very dated but comfy chairs and a couch, a small bedroom. His bed, where he was found unresponsive, was unmade. In his room, a layer of dust covered a picture of me at maybe six or seven years old. Now I was twenty-four, and a thousand other photos of me had been taken since that one. Why he had chosen to display that photo? Perhaps it was the age at which he wanted to remember me, when we still had some semblance of a relationship. There were no other photos in the apartment.

My uncle and I packed up boxes and took them out. We donated everything that we could.

He had to wear something in his casket. I chose a brown corduroy blazer, one that he was wearing in a photo from the 70s that I liked. He's standing at a bar with friends, smiling, with one of those chubby beer bottles in his hand, a boot up on the bar's foot rail. It is a really good photo of him, and besides, this was the only blazer he owned, even decades later. We found a pair of pants, a white-collared shirt, a red tie, and a pair of mismatched socks. He didn't have any matching socks that I could find, so that's what he was buried in.

We were packing things up, and I was setting aside things that I thought I might want to remember him by.

I came across a fire-safe box at the top of a bedroom closet. *Finally!* I thought. We had been sorting through all this stuff we'd never seen before that belonged to a man we didn't really know. Finding this box was like locating a black box in an airplane crash. There had to be some information here that could help us: a will, an unsent letter to me or my grandmother, something. Anything. That's what these types of boxes were for, after all.

But all that was in that box were his wedding band, an expired passport, a couple of loose coins, and a Post-it Note with instructions about what to do with his cat when he died. It was so disappointing.

We finished emptying the apartment. As we cleaned, his friends kept stopping by, each of them with stories about Bob. One of his best friends arrived, and he was broken up about my father's death. I asked him if he would help me pick the pall-bearers. He graciously offered more names than I needed and did so in rapid-fire fashion. The number of people he suggested and the speed at which he proffered his list took me aback.

At the funeral home a few days later, I barely recognized the man in the casket. Most people in the visitation line were his friends. They told my uncle and me about how great Bob was and how much they would miss him and how he had impacted their lives.

I kept thinking, *Who are they talking about?*

This was not the Bob I had known. A good guy? Someone fun to be around? Someone loyal and who always had their backs? *This can't be the man in the casket.*

Through all the numbness I experienced over the day of visitation and the funeral, it became crystal clear to me that I had very little to say about Bob because my relationship with him had been father–son, and he didn't fulfill his role.

However, those who had friend-friend relationships with him couldn't stop talking about him.

Even through all the reconciling of his death, I managed to recognize and appreciate the fact that while he wasn't much of a father, apparently he was one heck of a friend.

There's a magical time in many young people's lives when their relationship with their parents starts to shift, and if they're lucky, their parents become their friends, too. It's a beautiful harmony. Today, I love hanging out with my mother and my stepfather, just having a glass of wine and spending time with them. I can't help but wonder whether, if Bob had lived longer, we could have hit that stride. Could we have moved past the fractured nature of our relationship?

Could I have appreciated him the way his friends did?

No matter how different we are as people, as humans we have a lot in common. The human condition isn't as complicated as we often think it is.

Bob and I could have talked about plenty of things. We both loved art; we both loved friendships; we both had a fondness for simplicity. I learned that he was quite spiritual and that he enjoyed exploring deeper truth by conversing with friends, new and old.

But he died before we got to know each other, and there's nothing I can do about that. I can, however, take lessons from the way he lived.

My appreciation for Bob has shifted from the negative place of believing he wasn't a good father to the positive position of acknowledging that he was a good friend. A great friend.

People's lives were better because he was friends with them. Of that I'm sure, without hesitation.

Maybe he should not have been a father; but biology took over, which, as I live and breathe, I'm thankful for.

I don't know what Bob felt about being a father. Did he have issues, thinking he couldn't do the job well? Maybe he thought he wasn't good enough. Or that he would be a disappointment. I cry for the father he might have been, but I smile for the friend that he was—a friend I would have been happy to know. Rather than focusing on the things I did not love about him, I choose to see something that I can be proud of.

I think Bob knew he was a good friend and he played to his strengths. His friends were distraught when he died because they lost someone in their present. I was distraught because I lost my hope for a reconciled future with him.

My father lived a legacy of being a caring man. You can't be a great friend without having love in your heart. He was a bad father, but that doesn't mean he was a bad man. His friends cried at his funeral because he had lived his truth.

Having a funeral for Bob the father would not have been worth it, but having a funeral for Bob the man, the friend, was a celebration.

Hurt people, hurt people. Believing this helps you understand that their intentions aren't necessarily theirs, but a by-product of their own experience, being thrust upon you, perhaps even unconsciously.

In even the most fractured relationships, when we ask our ego to stand down for a moment, we may realize that there can be beauty in despair, hope in anguish, and ultimately light in the darkness. When the bad in people hurts you a lot, if you look hard enough, you can see the good. Even if the good that you're looking for exists in you because of that experience.

Sure, a part of me says, *Codi, what about you? He was supposed to be your father.* But what might have been isn't going to happen now.

I could have spent all the time between his funeral and today being bitter about our relationship, but I don't want that to be any part of my legacy. Bob deserves to be remembered for who he was.

For a lesson that could have breathed new life into our relationship when he was alive, how ironic is it that it was learned when there was no breath left in his body? The most important lesson I learned from my father came when one would suspect everything that could have been learned would already have been learned: at the end.

5

ECHOES OF REGRET

CHOICES ABOUT NOW

As a funeral director, I have sat around the arrangement table with thousands of people over the years. It's a very peculiar position to be with families at their most raw and vulnerable moments, yet to never really be part of the conversation. It's more like actively eavesdropping, while in the same room as the bereaved, and providing insights and guidance.

I can't count the number of times I've heard, "I wish I had..." or "I wish I hadn't said or done..."

"I wish I'd visited more... called more..."
"I wish I hadn't gone to bed angry."
"I should have said 'I love you.'"
"I shouldn't have had that argument."
"Why didn't I give them one more hug?"

And every time I heard such words uttered at that table, a voice echoed in my head that said, *Why didn't you?* or *Why did you?*

The sad truth is, most of the regrets I heard were about very manageable changes in behavior. Many could have been made in a split second. In the snap of a finger.

If we are behaving mindfully and living our Everyday Legacy authentically, our interactions have far more grace and consideration. Things like empathy are at play more commonly in our lives.

Because I want to live without regrets, I don't hang up from a phone call with my mother before telling her that I love her. There have been times when we've been on the phone and cut off for some reason, and I have called her back just to utter that sentence.

If I don't wake up in the morning, I want those to be the last words she hears from me.

My greatest fear isn't dying. My greatest fear is dying without being able to say goodbye.

Saying "I love you" is one of the ways I control that unknown variable, the big question mark of when.

Because I lived my entire career within arm's length of the awareness that tomorrow doesn't always come, I say I love you to people who mean something to me. As a funeral director, when you've been inundated with other people's echoes of regret, you become acutely aware of the last words you say to those you love. That's why I won't go to bed with arguments in the air.

A regret is something we wish we had done differently. Regrets will feed your ego and burden your conscience. But we have the power to avoid regrets.

To live without regret means to communicate with love and empathy. Although I openly tell people I love them, there are many ways to express love. Some people show their love through actions rather than words. Whether you're saying it or showing it through behavior, as long as it's consistent and congruent with what you want to be remembered for, you aren't going to live with echoes of regret.

Before someone is gone, you can prevent the *I should have*s and the *I wish I had*s. If you need to reach a resolution with someone you might otherwise attach a regret to, then you have to have those conversations now, before one or the other of you reach the end.

Otherwise, you end up in a situation like mine with my father: I can only *imagine* our relationship would have improved. How powerful might it have been if we'd had some important conversations while Bob was alive, about what we meant to each other and what we'd learned, how we felt? Who knows? We might have had a unique start to our father–son relationship and yet one that was profound in the end. It may or may not have gone this way, and I will never know. Death interrupted what could or might have been.

Every day, people bury their loved ones, and if they have regrets, these may well echo throughout their lives.

That awareness is powerful enough to shift how we behave. It should be enough to make you consider the effect of your words and gestures on everyone you encounter as you journey through life.

My Everyday Legacy is about impact, so that means doing my best to be kind and thoughtful at almost every juncture. It's taking an extra step to ask the frazzled server how their day is going, giving them a chance to catch their breath at my table. It's giving a hug, or telling a joke, or saying "I love you." It's opening a door or helping someone with their bags. It's the tiny, seemingly inconsequential things that can have such a massive effect on people.

Another way to compound that mindfulness and presence is to practice what I like to call "micro-acknowledgment": in essence, it's gratitude, but on a much more granular level. Gratitude might sound like a buzzword that people like to use, but for those who have a regular practice of honoring the meaningful things in their lives, gratefulness is powerful. For many years, I journaled about gratitude every day, but that came to feel more like a chore versus something I did because I craved giving my attention to the things I'm grateful for. I wanted to find a way to make my gratitude practice less task-based and "once-a-day," and more of a reflexive behavior that I could envelop throughout my daily interactions.

I now call this micro-acknowledgment. It's being thankful for things, often those same seemingly inconsequential things, in the moment. It's waking up and reminding myself to be thankful for the breath I draw. It's getting out of bed and being thankful for my mobility. It's reaching for the coffee maker and the fresh grounds to brew a pot of morning fuel and having a deep appreciation for all that, and the home I'm in to enjoy it. Sometimes, when I grumble about a lousy sleep or I groan as something aches when I start my day, it's also grounding to stop and realize that there are others in the world in a far less fortunate position, and this quickly adjusts my perspective.

I don't profess to go through every day, at every single moment, with an omnipresent practice of micro-acknowledgment. But

I do find that—to course-correct the ego and overtake the often-misguided advice it's trying hard to convince us of—considering things in the moment that we're thankful for is powerful. Especially when we notice our ego's voice grumbling often and far louder than it should.

If we all took just a moment to do some of these little things in our day, whether for others or even sometimes just for ourselves, how much better would humankind be?

Frequently, when we're doing things to limit echoes of regret, we realize that our acts of kindness, generosity of spirit, and philanthropic efforts have far more consequence for us than they do for the benefactors.

If everyone lived with purposeful empathy and compassion, it would be like an infection the world would be better for having contracted.

You can choose to be consciously aware now, or wait for perspective to bruise you, to remind you to be aware. Death will happen, and sometimes when it is least expected. When the end moves closer, if you're living consciously and purposefully, you can rest easy knowing your loved ones do not doubt that they mattered to you. Void of regret.

Let's live without regrets echoing in our minds and burdening our hearts and, at the end of each day, with awareness that we expressed what needed to be said and did what needed to be done.

We have little control over our death, but we're entirely in control of how we live.

6

MORTALITY

PERSPECTIVE AND LIVING WITH PURPOSE

P LEASE, DON'T *let it be cancer.*
That was the only thought racing through my mind as
I lost consciousness.

In the recovery room, several hours later, coming out
of anesthesia, I opened my eyes and blinked against the bright
light of the fluorescent tubes. Everything was a blur, except
for those lights. I felt unable to move. Sounds were muffled. I
didn't know if there were ten people in the room, or three, or if
I was alone. There was nothing but me and those lights.

But then someone was there, between the lights and me. I
could sense them coming closer. Suddenly, a nurse loomed
overhead, directly above my face, in my minuscule field of
vision. She placed a hand on my shoulder and, in a clear voice,
said, "Hi, Codi. Welcome back. The surgery is over. How do
you feel?"

I cared about only one thing, but I was afraid to ask the
question.

Was the undertaker in me more worried than he needed to
be? I had to find the courage to utter the words.

Her answer could change my life. I was terrified. The nurse knew the truth about the thing that had been keeping me awake at night.

I squinted to focus on her face. My mouth was dry, but I managed to say it: "Do I have cancer?"

I braced myself.

The nurse said, "We ran a biopsy of the tumor during surgery, and while the results aren't 100 percent, they're very close. We'll be sending it off for more testing, but the doctor is confident that no, you don't have cancer. Now, how are you feeling?"

Relief surged through every fiber of my being, and as I focused again on her face, I said the only thing that came to mind: "Who cares."

I didn't care if my leg felt as if it was falling off. I didn't care about the pounding migraine I had from the anesthetic. At that moment, I cared about nothing except the answer to that question.

It all happened so fast: the doctor's appointment, the MRI, the surgery. It was as though a tornado came out of nowhere, and I could see it off in the field, heading for my house. Everything and everyone that mattered to me was inside that house, and the storm was racing straight at it. The day of the surgery, right before I drifted off from the anesthetic, the tornado had arrived at my property line, looming—and when I woke up, in one sentence, the tornado disappeared.

My reaction was simple because, in that moment, everything inside me needed something to be uncomplicated.

Nothing had been so in the months leading up to the surgery. But as soon as I said the words, "Who cares," I realized that this was one of the few times in my life that I *did* care. A lot. About a lot of people and a lot of things. More than I had known.

Little did I suspect, however, that not having cancer would change my life almost as profoundly as if the tumor had not been benign.

Let me be clear. I am very aware of how fortunate I am that this cancer scare was only that: a scare. I can't imagine what people go through when they're delivered the kind of news that I had dreaded, and how life-altering that would be.

All I know is that, in the blink of an eye, I was inspired to live more bravely and more beautifully than I would have had I not been brushed by this experience.

I was a funeral director and an embalmer. I'd been surrounded by dead people for almost ten years by the time I had that cancer scare. How had I never before faced my own mortality? I honestly hadn't thought about it, until this happened and I had a horrible sense that maybe the tumor was cancer, that perhaps I would die.

The details of the scare itself aren't crucial to my story. But the very instant I heard the nurse's response, I decided that, for as long as I was afforded life, I would focus only on what is important, and the rest I would let go.

Although it sounds odd, I'm grateful for that cancer scare. It was the Universe delivering me a wallop in the face, which I needed to put things into perspective.

PERSPECTIVE AND PURPOSE

How many times have you said that some tragic event or news story helped put things into perspective? You're having a bad day. Maybe you had a negative experience at work or your car's battery died or an event you'd been looking forward to was canceled. Maybe you're feeling angry or sad or anxious. And then, on the news, you hear a story about people who are having a far worse day than you—there's a devastating natural disaster or a tragic accident. Or, even worse, you hear about a loved one receiving a scary health prognosis.

What happens then? Does your perspective shift? I'm willing to bet that you're nodding yes.

If you're self-aware on any level, this has probably happened to you at least once or twice. Maybe more times than that. Those moments remind you that your situation isn't so bad after all.

When crummy news fills our ears or a scene of sadness grazes our hearts, we tend to harness perspective and hold it close and tight. We promise that we won't let it out of our grip, clinging to it like something precious we lost long ago and have just found. We lose perspective and then grasp for dear life when we discover it again, because when we stand objectively and look at the world, we see a clearer picture, and our place in the grand scheme of things reveals itself just a little bit more.

When we have perspective, we take the time to call our loved ones more often, do the things we enjoy, and appreciate the beauty in life. We promise that we'll never again take the people and things we love for granted.

Why is it that we need some horrible revelation—a sudden accident, an awful diagnosis, or the death of a loved one—to pause... to break... to gain perspective on what's important to us, and moreover, *who* is important to us?

We're so consumed by the busyness of the day—work, family commitments, appointments, what to make for dinner—that we forget to appreciate every single moment and enjoy the journey. We spend too much time inside ourselves, where our egos live. Although hearing about tragic events often makes us aware of how lucky we are, usually that's not enough to push us to change in a long-term, sustainable way.

It's not long before our moods are once again influenced by the mundane: the dull meetings you dread; the day-to-day work grind; the never-ending, overwhelming pile of tasks that stack up. We stop checking in with our loved ones as often. No more time for lunch dates with our friends. We don't devote quite as much time to the activities and people we love. We complain about things that, when we had the slightest bit of perspective, we never would have grumbled about.

In my experience, minor stings such as hearing about the difficulties of others, do nothing. Perspective needs to hit so hard that it leaves a bruise. When perspective bruises us, it may be enough to wake us up, to make us consistently pay attention.

None of us is getting out of here alive. Yet until we're bruised by perspective, life tends to happen around us, and we lose sight of the things that don't directly affect us. We're so invested in our habits and routines that we forget about the value and importance of others. This is called "life taking over," and it happens to all of us—even those who are acutely conscious of this on a daily basis—until a grounding blow from perspective wakes us to the fact that we're mortal.

So, what does this bruise look like? Well, that's going to be different for every person. For me, it was a cancer scare. For others, a loved one might pass away before they have the chance to reconcile. Someone might lose a job or a relationship. Whatever that bruising moment is for us, it causes a shift that nudges us toward the truth, a deeper awareness of where we need to be.

But what if nothing in life bruises you? Or what if that grounding blow from perspective—that knockout punch—shatters some illusions you had about life, and you don't know what to do next?

You can find your truth by imagining that death is upon you and asking yourself one simple question: "What do I want to be remembered for?"

You might think this sounds rather daunting, or even macabre.

Do you really have to think about your own death to find truth?

Yes. You do. But this isn't about obsessing over your death. I am proposing that you bring your awareness to the end for just a moment. Think about how you want to be remembered, let yourself experience what comes up, and then come back to the present. That simple exercise can give you the perspective you need.

It isn't easy or fun or pleasant to think about death, but if you want to make your time here truly count, you have to understand that it's limited.

If you look at death through the lens I'm proposing, you'll start living with more intent and curiosity. You'll live knowing that when your last breath comes, you've lived on purpose, honestly, and without regret.

As you'll recall, your legacy doesn't refer to cars and boats, real estate and jewelry. Do you want to be remembered for the material things you've accumulated? Your legacy comprises qualities and characteristics. You may want to be remembered for bringing people together. For your generosity. For being there for those who need you. For always having a kind word. For making people smile.

Once you identify what you want your Everyday Legacy to be, how you want to be remembered, you'll have found the magic equation, the framework for how you live with perspective. And you'll live with such intent that between now and the end, your legacy will be written into the hearts of everyone around you.

7

TEA WITH THE QUEEN

ABOVE ALL ELSE, LOVE

ON JULY 17, 2009, I saw my grandmother on the subway.

Some might say, "That's nice" or "Big deal."

Either way, it is. She died in 2005.

Lulled by the rocking of the subway, I glanced right, and there she was, a woman in her seventies, standing, swaying, waiting to arrive at her destination.

She looked remarkably like my grandmother, only she appeared to be of African descent and my grandmother was European. But the shape of her face, her eyes, her hair—even the way she stood—it was as if my grandmother were there again, not ten feet away.

I thought of this woman's family. I hoped that she was loved. I hoped that they appreciated her. I hoped that her family, if she had one, cherished every moment they had with her. I know I did. My grandmother was an incredible human being. Together, we created memories that keep her very alive in my heart and mind forever. She was a strong woman, determined, loving, and real.

As my glance became a stare, the subway car slowed to a stop, and having arrived at her station, the woman turned and left the train. I smiled spontaneously. I had experienced another moment—though at a distance and only in my mind—with someone who meant so much to me.

When I arrived at my destination, instead of hastily racing up the left side of the escalator, I stood on the right side and paused, enjoying the ride, reminiscing and smiling the whole way.

What an incredible way to start the day.

Besides my mother, my grandmother has been the most important person in my life. She was my best friend. I often thought of myself as a weird kid and didn't feel I fit in anywhere, but I always fit in with her. Many children like spending time with their grandparents, but I *loved* it. We would routinely go to play minigolf or go swimming at a local beach. We were inseparable. She was so easygoing and lovely. I know now that she was trying to fill the gap that her son left in my life, which only expanded my love for her.

Pat was short for Patricia, and she had been born into affluence. Her family owned a private school in England. Growing up, I certainly felt as if my grandmother was royalty. It didn't hurt that she was British, and the accent helped, too. During our visits, we bonded over tea, toast, and bacon. But her affluent lifestyle ended by the time she was eight years old, when the family business was overtaken during the Second World War. Her father died after "mysteriously" falling through one of the school's second-story windows.

This marked the beginning of a very dark period in my grandmother's life. She didn't talk much about the years before she immigrated to Canada. But it must have been so jarring to go from wealth to poverty so quickly, from drinking tea in fine china to eating tulip bulbs to stay alive.

If someone were to have asked her eight-year-old self to sleep on anything but the finest linens, she would probably have thought that unacceptable. But the grandmother I loved would say, "If you have a sheet to cover you, be thankful for the sheet."

If you asked her eight-year-old self whether anything but the finest china was acceptable, she would say no. But the grandmother I loved drank her tea from the simplest of mugs.

My grandmother had such a warm, open heart. She loved deeply and lived simply.

"Simple" is a subjective word. Some people think that instant coffee in a pottery mug makes the simplest cup of coffee. Some say a simply made cup should be prepared with freshly ground beans and served only in fine bone china. Without a basis of comparison, it's tough to measure where you stand on a scale of simplicity.

Without that basis, it's tough to get perspective.

Imagine standing with your nose against a wall and seeing only brown. The world would be dark. But if you take a step back, you would see the outline of bricks. A few more steps back and you could count the bricks. More steps back and you could see the beautiful bright horizon over the top of the wall. Your world is no longer dark.

Some people go through life with their noses stuck to that wall, without knowing there's something more to be gained with just a bit of perspective.

My grandmother went from being so close to the wall that her nose touched it to eating tulip bulbs. Early in her life, circumstances gave her perspective on what was important, and that wasn't things.

It was immensely important to her to have character and integrity, a quiet conviction, and a servant's heart. And, above all else, to love deeply.

Many of us are blessed, and don't have the jarring experience of going from having everything to having nothing. Most of us have far more than we think. Some of us go through life with our noses on the wall, not seeing anything but brown. Not knowing what the wall is constructed of, or how tall or wide it is. Not being able to see past it, whatever that wall represents.

At the time of Grandma Pat's death, I felt so angry that I had only twenty-seven years with her. She died so young. There was so much life in her, but dementia had other plans.

Now, however, her life and the perspective dealt to me by her death have taught me to see things differently.

I recall reading an analogy that resonated profoundly with me. If I offered you $86,400, would you accept it from me?

What if I put a condition on that deal, and said that you have to spend all the money by the end of the day? It won't gain interest, you can't bank it, and it won't carry over to tomorrow.

I'm guessing that you would jump at this offer and choose to make the most out of each of those dollars. You wouldn't waste a single one, because you'd know you'll lose them if you don't use them!

The thing is, we are given this amount each day—that is, 86,400 *seconds*. We can't bank what we don't use, and we can't carry the balance forward. Every time the clock strikes midnight, our bank is refilled.

This means that I had my grandmother for 851,472,000 seconds. If seconds with her were dollars, I was a very rich man.

Time is a currency we're all afforded. Until we're not. We do well to spend our seconds wisely.

I would jump at the chance for another second. One more cup of tea. One more game of minigolf. But I can choose to focus on the gratitude I have for what was, rather than dwell on what I wish for that can't ever be.

The night Grandma Pat died, I was there, holding her hand. When she departed from this world, she left me with some of the richest experiences I will ever have, the most important lessons I will ever learn, and sweet memories that I treasure and turn to daily.

For as long as I want, I have a standing date to remember the lessons my grandmother taught me. I think of it as tea with the queen. My queen.

I inherited my grandmother's original Brown Betty teapot. Every time I reach for it, it's as though I'm inviting her to sit with me. All I have to do is pour a cup of tea and pause to remember her, how she lived simply but with conviction, with a heart filled with love. I can have that forever.

8

PAUSE

TIME TO CREATE MEANING

HAVE YOU ever walked into a big-box store looking for a seasonal item—a bag of salt for your icy front step, say—only to pass displays of unseasonal items such as spring bulbs and topsoil along the way?

In the world of competitive retail commerce, Christmas decorations are up before the Halloween candy and costumes are put away. Valentine's Day chocolates hit the shelves the minute Christmas is dismantled. You can find back-to-school sales before the kids are even out of class for the summer.

If you took people who had been living in isolation, dropped them into one of these stores, and asked them what time of year it was, they would probably guess wrong.

"Surely it must be spring. There's an Easter display!"

No, it's January.

When I was a kid, you had to get to the drive-through before 11 a.m. if you wanted to order a breakfast sandwich. Not anymore! You can get breakfast all day long.

The internet has given us the ability to work around the clock. The world no longer operates on Monday-to-Friday, nine-to-five business hours. Those are archaic. We check our e-mails before we go to bed, first thing in the morning, and at all points in between.

We eat our microwaved dinners standing at the kitchen counter at 9 p.m., scrolling through our social media feeds or catching up on our recorded TV shows. Do you remember the days when you had to read the printed *TV Guide* to find out what was on, and then sit and watch precisely at the time your show aired? In the days before on-demand television, e-mail, and microwaves, we certainly had a different awareness of time, didn't we? We were slower, because the world hadn't yet given us a faster, more convenient, more efficient way of doing just about everything.

Time is no longer delineated. Breaks and rituals do not punctuate our days.

No wonder we're all in such a hurry. No wonder we have such problems setting boundaries and turning the switch off. So many people do not have a switch!

We don't stop for lunch, we grab whatever we can find, whenever we can tear ourselves away from our work. We don't stop to cook dinner. We eat whatever's convenient, whenever we can fit it into our busy lives. We have no need to curl up in front of the evening news because we've been reading the news all day long.

These days, time is just something nobody seems to have enough of.

When I was a child, you could set your watch by teatime at my grandmother's house. No matter what was going on, at 3 p.m., my grandmother stopped what she was doing and put on the kettle.

To my grandmother, tea wasn't just a drink. It was much bigger than that. Tea meant taking a break, carving out fifteen minutes, sometimes several times a day, oftentimes alone, for my grandmother to check in with herself. Teatime was for her. You might ask how much time a person needs when she spends the majority of her time alone. Well, my grandmother used her teatime to be active in her solitude.

Tea was her pause, a time to stop and think about what was important that day. Sometimes she would make phone calls and check in with her loved ones. When she had visitors, tea was about time together. Tea was a ritual, and with that came conversation and reflection.

My grandmother knew the difference between efficiency and effectiveness. For her, there was no such thing as an efficient way to make tea; there was only an effective way. Can you make tea by dropping a tea bag into a mug of water and putting it in the microwave for ninety seconds? You can, sure. But, according to her, that's not going to make a delicious cup of tea.

A drive-through car wash is efficient, but you might enjoy the therapeutic process of washing your car by hand.

Ordering takeout is an adequate way to put dinner on the table, but a great satisfaction comes with preparing a meal from scratch yourself.

Sending a friend a text message to see how they're doing is an economic use of time, but it's not quite the same as picking up the phone and talking.

As a society, we are consumed by efficiency, collectively racing from one thing to the other and from one person to the next. Being able to make the rush seem effortless is perceived as honorable. Those who work the most are revered, as though the most stressed-out person will be awarded a trophy.

Sometimes you have to choose the efficient way; there's no denying that. But we could all try a little harder to choose the effective way more often, especially when it comes to our relationships.

How do we do that when we are in the throes of the hustle? We pause.

Most of life's magic happens in moments of pause. We need to stop and re-center in order to reach a state of conscious awareness. Pausing helps us to slow down and plan our time more effectively, so that we create more meaning in our lives. The way my grandmother did with her tea.

One morning, while I was in the middle of writing this book, I had a 10 a.m. phone meeting scheduled. The person I was speaking with could tell there was something different about my voice. I'd slept in. I'd been working long hours and not getting enough rest. She asked me if I was sick.

I paused and said, "No, I actually just got out of bed not too long ago, and I guess my voice just hasn't woken up yet."

Would you admit to sleeping until almost ten in the morning on a Wednesday?

Many people would make something up: "Oh, I've been up for hours! You're right, I must be coming down with something!"

Why?

I know my body well enough to sense when I need to stop. But we're so programmed to think we have to go, go, go that we sometimes feel shame in taking time to pause ... as though there were a negative connotation to slowing down.

I'm not saying the hustle isn't important. It is. When you're in business, you need some hustle. When you're an athlete, the hustle is essential. Hustling hard can be a good thing. But working hard and working smart are very different things, and working smart is the better choice.

Working smart creates room; it puts equal emphasis on the hustle and the pause. And if you don't pause, you may fall out of alignment with yourself and get lost as a result.

Think of a ship that drifts one degree off course. Nobody notices one degree. What's one degree? But when one degree adds to another, and then to another, and you realize you're forty degrees off track with no idea where you're going, then you have a problem.

This is what can happen when we're too focused on the hustle.

I entered the hustle at a young age. I was in my very early twenties when I started my corporate career, and I succeeded in moving through various positions quite quickly. I was managing a facility and a team by the age of twenty-three. Eventually, I was managing different locations. At twenty-seven years old, I was head of a national leadership development program and traveling a lot. It was a hectic lifestyle—no question. And as much as it fulfilled me because it was my passion, over time, when a lot of aspects of my life became secondary to the hustle, my job became soul-crushing.

We can't go nine hundred miles an hour in all areas of life at all times. We can hustle in one lane, but while we're doing that, we have to slow down in the others. It's the law of balance. So often with hustle, we lack balance, and then we have to create it manually. It's not automatic.

Part of living your Everyday Legacy is recognizing when there's an imbalance, when work is taking priority and occupying times that perhaps used to be filled with family or conversation. Pause is about creating non-negotiables—areas of life that you don't compromise, no matter what. If that's family time, then you make sure nothing interferes with it. If it's calling someone on a regular basis, you honor the time and space for that to happen. If it's saying you'll do something, you do it.

Legacy is a matter of how you show up. When that starts to shift for the worse, you have an imbalance, a sign that you're off course, and it's time to pause.

For me, a pause can be as simple as making a cup of tea. Sometimes it's lighting a candle and sitting alone with my thoughts in a quiet room. Other times it's hopping in the pool even though there's work to be done. Sometimes it's sleeping in when I am tired. I've gone off course, and I don't want that to happen again, so I've learned to pause when I need to.

Be it meditation, taking time to connect with someone whose values you admire, getting in a workout, cooking your favorite meal, or something else, the activity itself isn't as important as identifying that you need a pause, and taking one.

Life happens in those moments when you pay attention, when you're mindful of what's going on in front of you. Although it doesn't matter what you do to pause, you need to get something from the activity—a connection or meaning that is much larger than whatever you're doing. Forget about multitasking. It's impossible to give more than one thing your full attention. Allot your full focus to the activity of your pause.

Pausing helps us stay centered and be authentic. If you're attempting to live your values, making sure they're infused in your very essence, you have to live mindfully.

It's often in the quiet times, when we have conversations with only ourselves, that life reveals itself. The more we make time and space to contemplate what's important to us and how we're showing up in the world, the more we perceive recurring themes. Perhaps we are reminded that we want graciousness, generosity, or reliability to be our legacy. Without these conversations in moments of pause, be they ten minutes or ten hours long, we move further from our truth and from showing up authentically each day.

When you distill it down, why you go back to the teakettle or the gym or the dog park—or wherever you go to pause—becomes clear. The activity purposefully feeds you. It fills your cup. And to be of service to others, you need your cup to be full, so you have enough for yourself; what overflows is for everyone else.

9

ASHRAM

ALLOWING FOR THE UNEXPECTED

VEN THOUGH I was living the life I thought I wanted, hard-core into the hustle, climbing my company's corporate ladder faster and higher than anyone else my age, something inside me was nudging me to slow down. I had this feeling that I needed to take a break, to do something that would shake myself outside my comfort zone. The more I thought about it, the more this feeling graduated to a need, and I knew it was time.

I was sitting at my desk when I had a crazy idea. I love to travel, so I decided . . . *I'm going to book a vacation and go somewhere I've never been before, without planning ahead.*

Up until then, all my experience with travel had been very prescriptive, much like my life. I would book tickets and spend weeks planning, researching, and packing. But this time, I was going to push myself. I was going to choose a random destination and be on a plane within twenty-four hours. I was going to ditch the type-A, anal-retentive, plan-every-teeny-tiny-detail Codi, and welcome a version of myself that previously I had only caught a glimpse of.

I picked up the phone, called a travel agent, and said, "I would like to go on a trip anywhere in the world, for up to seven days. I have a decent budget, and I need to leave tomorrow. Where should I go?"

Silence on the other end of the phone. And then the agent said, "Where would you *like* to go?"

"Anywhere in the world. Doesn't matter."

"Umm... I need to put something into the system. Can you give me some ideas? Within Canada? The United States?"

"No, you don't understand. I want *you* to tell *me* where I should go. It can be anywhere, as long as I can leave within twenty-four hours."

More silence.

The travel agent could not fathom what I was asking, and after several minutes of back-and-forth, we were both getting frustrated. Then, out of nowhere, my mind drifted to a trip I'd taken to the Bahamas about a year before, and I remembered passing a yoga place on a beach walk one day and being intrigued by what I could see as I walked by. *That's it*, I thought. *I want to go there.*

I now understand that this was the Universe tapping me on the shoulder, nudging me back to that yoga center. I was not very self-aware at the time, but... I was happy this idea occurred to me.

I hung up the phone, did some internet research, quickly found the yoga retreat I'd been thinking of, and immediately called for information.

As it turned out, a three-day program with the theme of abandoning the ego was coming up.

I didn't know what "abandoning the ego" meant, but I asked the pleasant lady on the other end of the line to please sign me up. It was 3 p.m. I booked myself a flight for the following day at seven in the morning.

DAY ONE

I was pacing back and forth on the dock, waiting for a boat to pick me up and take me to the place . . . an ashram, whatever that was. I couldn't believe I had actually gone through with this. Normally, I would have planned a trip like this for months. But here I was. In the Bahamas. Twelve hundred miles from home and about twelve million miles outside my comfort zone.

From the dock, I could see the high-end hotel complex and resort where I'd stayed when I'd previously visited the Bahamas. Five-star everything. Luxury at every turn. A place that smells like money. I had a feeling my second time to the islands would be different. I'd be lucky if there was Wi-Fi where I was heading.

Wait . . . What if there's no internet?

Can anybody reach me on my cell? Am I completely disconnected from the world?

Where is the boat? It should have been here by now. Am I at the right place?

So many questions.

There's not even a sign.

All the lady at the ashram had said was to tell the taxi driver to drop me off at the ashram's pickup dock, and that the driver would know where that was. Other than that, I had zero frame of reference. I wondered if I had missed the boat, and what I had gotten myself into.

How disconnected will I be from civilization?

Finally, I spotted a boat. A *small* boat. Was it coming for me? As it drew closer, the man behind the wheel waved.

I guess this is it. There's no turning back now, Codi.

Breathe.

After a five-minute boat ride, during which I was alone in the boat with the man, who barely said anything beyond "Hello," we floated up to a dock. He welcomed me to the retreat and, as he tied up the boat, pointed me toward a path that led to what looked like a jungle. I noticed a colorful sign with an arrow pointing to a path, and assumed I was supposed to follow it.

It was so hot and humid that my clothes were drenched in sweat. I stepped onto the path and the open Caribbean sky disappeared behind dense foliage. Tropical birds sang. The vegetation was lush and full.

All I could think was . . . *I'm starving.*

Nobody was around and I was beginning to worry that I'd signed up for a self-directed program until, through the trees, I glimpsed someone dressed completely in orange.

Okay, I'm not here alone.

I found the welcome center, which was more of a welcome hut—a white, shed-like building with a small window and counter, enough space inside to turn around, and that was about all.

The staff member who greeted me handed me a schedule before escorting me to my room. She was very kind and smiled while she told me about the property, gesturing to the dining area and washrooms as we passed by.

Maybe this won't be quite as dismal as I thought.

I was trying to have an open mind, but the place was a lot to take in, especially since I hadn't done any research. Although the temperature was jarring, it wasn't so much the environment that was challenging me. It was not knowing . . . anything.

Even though it was so hot I could barely breathe as we walked along, hope sprung up. I was looking forward to seeing the beautiful room that awaited me on the other side of the door I was being led to. A few people milled about, some of whom, I learned, were yogis. The woman leading me told me they were doing karma yoga as part of their teacher training. They were working, some of them in silence. Some prepared meals, some performed painting duties, some were raking up the jungle's natural debris. Around the property, they quietly toiled, but I still seemed to be the only workshop participant on the grounds.

This quiet is so dense, it's almost deafening.

As we weaved our way down one path and then another, my excitement about seeing my room grew. Along the way, I was taken by the surroundings. The property was quite beautiful, with the overgrown plants and flowers.

Finally, we stopped in front of a door on the ground level of a larger building. My anticipation was mounting! She inserted the key, turned the handle, and opened the door to my room, and . . .

Wow. Okay . . . This is . . . quaint?

With a small window and a tiny, open closet beside the door, the entire room was the size of my walk-in closet at home. The staff person left me to organize my things, which was good, because the room was too tiny for two people to be in it at the same time. There was barely enough space for me and my suitcase. I sat down on the bed. The mattress was so hard, I thought it was made of wood. I pulled out the retreat schedule and had a look:

5:30 A.M. WAKE UP

6 A.M. TO 8 A.M. MORNING MEDITATION

8 A.M. TO 10 A.M. YOGA

10 A.M. BREAK FOR VEGAN BRUNCH

NOON TO 2 P.M. PROGRAMMING

2 P.M. TO 4 P.M. REFLECTIVE FREE TIME

4 P.M. TO 6 P.M. YOGA

6 P.M. VEGAN DINNER

8 P.M. TO 10 P.M. MEDITATION

10 P.M. LIGHTS OUT

GUESTS ARE ENCOURAGED NOT TO SPEAK BETWEEN EVENING MEDITATION AND 8 A.M. YOGA.

I made some quick calculations: that was four hours of meditation and four hours of yoga per day, two yogi-prepared vegan meals, and tea and water to drink.

My stomach dropped as I stared at the sheet in my hand, my anxiety growing the longer I looked at it. *What have I signed up for?* I'd be eating twice a day, and I had yet ever to set foot in a yoga studio, and now I would be expected to do yoga for four hours a day? Quiet my mind for another four hours a day? It basically sounded impossible. The only things I had experience with were the tea and water.

I unpacked the three or four articles of clothing I had brought along with me and hung them up. It was early afternoon, and I was free until 4 p.m. I put on a swimsuit and ventured to the beach.

The beach was as deserted as the ashram grounds. Hardly anyone came here at this time of year. No wonder: it was blisteringly hot. And it was hurricane season.

I felt as though I was already losing weight. Between the ten pounds I must have sweat off that day and the fact that all I'd eaten was a pack of pretzels, I was fading away. According to the schedule, I'd missed brunch, and since it didn't appear the ashram had a secret midafternoon all-you-can-eat buffet, I would have to wait until dinner.

And I still had yoga to get through.

Did I come all this way to starve to death in the jungle and pay them for the experience?

As far as I could see, there was nothing around but beach, ocean, and jungle for miles. Except, off in the distance, that luxury hotel resort I had stayed at before beckoned.

Hmm. They have food. They have drinks. It's not far...

Stop it, Codi! You're here to do this, and you're going to do this. It's not supposed to be comfortable.

I dipped into the perfectly blue, pristine water. *This is nice, like a giant bathtub.* I swam for a while before finding my way to a spot on the sand.

On the beach, I spotted a woman who looked out of place at a yoga retreat. She had the full beach getup: wide-brimmed hat, big sunglasses, bikini, fancy towel. I would have expected to see her at an all-inclusive resort, not ... here. Was she lost? Did she not realize the resort was two miles up the beach? She looked up from her magazine when I passed, and I said hello.

I was nervous about yoga.

At least I had my pants. Oh, my pants. After booking my flight the day before, I had rushed to a yoga-clothing retailer just to buy those pants and have them adjusted so that I could look the part. They seemed like such a good idea in the store. Back in my room before class, not so much. I hadn't considered how hot it was going to be. Yoga shorts might have been smarter. I squeezed into the tight black pants and left my room for the blinding jungle heat.

By the time I arrived at the yoga room, I was drenched in sweat.

I wish I were wearing shorts.

I noticed the woman from the beach and placed my mat beside hers, introducing myself. She told me her name was Molly.

The yogi said, "For the first day of the retreat, we will be doing basic sun salutations."

I considered raising my hand to ask what a sun salutation was, but we'd already started. The movement did *not* feel basic to me. Nothing about this felt basic.

For two hours, I thought, *I have no business being here.*

The instructor corrected me what felt like a million times. She told me to lean this way and point that way and squeeze this and stretch that, and focus on my breath, which was funny, because I couldn't catch my breath long enough to focus on it.

By the end of it, I was drenched in sweat again.

But ... I did it.

It was almost over. We'd been instructed to lie on the floor for our final pose, something called *savasana*. She told us to tense every muscle in our bodies and then relax, become one with the floor. In a rhythmic chant, the yogi encouraged us to relax each body part, from our heads all the way to our toes. Tense, and relax. Tense, and relax. "Every time you hear the word 'relax,'" she said, "deepen into the relaxation more and sink further and further, letting every tension go."

This feels good. Like, really good.

Is that what doing nothing feels like? I stared at the ceiling only to realize I couldn't remember the last time I had stopped and done nothing. I experienced the presence of my body and my mind, together.

I think I can live through this.

By the end of class, dinner was ready, and I was soaked with sweat. I dropped my mat off at my room and thought about hitting the shower. But no, people were eating already. I had to drag my disgusting, sweaty self to the dining area. Everything about that day had been uncomfortable, so why should that change now?

At the tables where the food was laid out, I picked up my metal plate, cup, and utensils.

These look like the prison dishes I see on TV.

I fully expected to be served a ration of slop. But the food looked delicious and healthy. What any of it was, was a mystery to me, but it smelled amazing. I scooped up a portion I thought I could eat and spotted Molly, and asked if I could join her for dinner. She was sitting near two other women: Taryn from Maryland and Sophie from New Mexico, who were busy catching up. These two friends had met up for a yoga vacation. I took a place at the table across from Molly.

After talking with her for five minutes, it was clear she was more into the hustle than I was. She lived in the heart of Manhattan. She was a movie producer who supplemented her income by working at a bar in the financial district. She was *Sex and the City* personified. I liked her immediately. This wasn't her first yoga and meditation experience, and when Molly told me I'd be fine, and to give it my all, I decided to heed her advice. I tried to be optimistic.

In the evening—after showering—I stepped into the temple for meditation. That I felt immediately uncomfortable didn't surprise me. After all, I'd never meditated before, so I didn't know what it was supposed to look or feel like, or anything. The lights were out, but four little candles glowed in the room. Everyone was sitting in that classic yoga pose, cross-legged, palms up. It was dead silent. Some people had their eyes closed, but some turned to note that I'd entered the room. Nobody spoke.

I took a seat and crossed my legs.

I want to close my eyes, but I'm not sure if I'm supposed to. I might miss something.

Silence.

I can't hear myself think, it's so quiet.

More silence.

I was getting a bit freaked out.

Images of Hindu deities on the walls stared at me, almost creepily, in the candlelight.

I closed my eyes.

A bell chimed.

I opened my eyes. What was happening? From somewhere in the room, a throaty gurgle swelled up: *ooouuummm.*

What is that?!

Others joined in.

Am I supposed to make that sound? Does that sound mean something? Is it another language? What is happening?!

A woman began to play an instrument that looked as though a piano and an accordion had a baby, and the room erupted with chanting in a language I didn't recognize.

Many people seemed to know the melody, and some knew the words. The chant had a catchy, melodic sound, but it made me feel even more like the odd one out.

Is this what not doing any research gets me?

Shouldn't someone have told us what to do here?

This was a big mistake.

I tried to steady my breath and looked around at other people. They didn't seem panicked or scared. Molly, although not united with others in chanting, sat with a pleasant smile playing at the corners of her lips.

She seems fine, and she's done this before.

I followed her lead, tried to relax and push through the unknown, and focused on the chanting.

Remember why you're here, Codi. To slow down. Let life happen.

I decided to close my eyes and concentrate on the sounds: the words, the music, the bells, the *ooouuummms.* I visualized a sponge soaking up water. I was the sponge. The experience was water.

Finally, somehow, I lost track of time and arrived at a place of calm. Before I knew it, it was the end of the two-hour meditation session.

Back in my room, I was completely exhausted.

At 10 p.m., the ashram shut down. It was dead silent. Pitch-black.

As I crawled into bed, my mind wandered back to the last couple of hours in the temple. I reflected on how the meditation lesson, which I had expected we'd receive as a formal set of verbal instructions, seemed to have been communicated without words.

Maybe it's about not needing to know everything.

My left brain kicked in: *But how do I gauge my results? Did I have any?*

In my work life, I was supposed to show results. The meditation session just left me with questions: *Had I been successful? Did it work? Could I have done it better? What could I have done differently?*

The heat continued to be as thick as the darkness of the night. My body was ready to sleep, but my brain had different ideas, and my thoughts raced until, eventually, I drifted off.

DAY TWO

A bell tolled. Not a nice, eloquent bell with a cheerful chime, but rather one like an old, rusty triangle and a cast-iron pot clanging together. I peeked out of my room into the darkness, and sure enough, the ringing was purposeful. The shadow of a person hauled away ferociously at the triangle, with one sole intention: to let everyone on the ashram property, or perhaps the entire island, know that it's thirty minutes until temple. Get up. Get showered. Get ready.

I felt more comfortable entering the temple on day two because I knew what to expect, and I was reasonably sure no humans would be sacrificed there.

Others had arrived before me. I didn't see Taryn or Sophie, but Molly was there. I sat near her, crossed my legs, and tried to focus on the silence.

My thoughts drifted to work, and e-mails, and how I had not checked in with the real world for twenty-four hours.

I am not good at meditating.

As with the night before, the first thirty minutes were entirely silent, and it felt like hours passed, sitting in the dark in total silence. When the chanting began, instead of being swept up by the unfamiliarity of the situation, I realized just how mesmerizing it was. I was beginning to relax.

I am here, and I might as well do this. My plane ticket back isn't for another couple of days, so this is me. Committing. I'm all in.

I could feel myself beginning to surrender to the experience.

After meditation, we were right into yoga. Taryn and Sophie arrived and set down their mats near Molly and me.

Day two's yogi didn't seem quite as laid-back as day one's. He meant business.

I thought the day before had been uncomfortable, but I was about to experience next-level discomfort. All I could do was lean into the familiarities of yesterday to ground my mind and go with the experience.

As the yogi talked us through contortions and manipulations of our bodies, I listened, trying to breathe and follow along. He walked around the room, methodically telling us what to do and monitoring our attention to his words.

Okay, he's giving us actual instructions. If I just do what he says, maybe I'll get somewhere. Instructions, I can follow.

I was on my knees, on the mat, facing forward.

I leaned forward to put my forearms on the mat ahead of me, shoulder width apart, and cupped my fingers.

I placed the crown of my head in the cup of my hands. Slowly, I shifted the weight of my body, distributed it evenly through my shoulders and arms, and lifted my legs, stopping midway to center my body and my balance. Once balanced, I popped my legs up to vertical.

Am I doing a headstand?! Wow! I'm in a headstand! This is cool.

I took a deep breath in, let a deep breath out, held the position, and carefully, when it felt right, reversed each of the steps until I was back down on the mat.

As I came out of the pose, I noticed Sophie struggling. The yogi encouraged her to be patient and persist.

"I need the wall," she said. "I've done yoga for years. I know I can't do a headstand without the wall."

"You don't need the wall," the yogi said. "Just do it."

"I can't do it! I need the wall!" I could tell she was getting frustrated.

The yogi pulled Sophie's mat to the middle of the room. "You don't need the wall. Just get down and do it. You've done yoga before. Great. Along with that, you have it preconstructed in your mind that you need the wall, but you don't."

This yogi was hard-core. Downright militant. A militant yogi. It struck me that he might be a walking, talking oxymoron.

He pointed to me and said sternly, "You. How long have you been doing yoga?"

"This is my first time," I answered, not really knowing the intent of his question.

"That's why he did a headstand," the yogi told Sophie. "He had no preconceived notion about it being difficult. He didn't know using the wall might be an option. His ego has had no time to construct a reason for him not to be able to do a headstand. Your ego is telling you that you can't do it, but you can. Your mind is limiting your ability. Your ego is in control."

Her mat was front and center, and it didn't look as if she had much choice but to do this.

I felt embarrassed for Sophie. The yogi was singling her out, making an example of her. She must have felt awful. I hoped he was doing this to show us a lesson. If not, it was mean, which didn't seem congruent with the spirit of the ashram and my experience to that point.

Was it because I was a newbie that I could do the headstand? On the fitness spectrum, I was not the most in shape in the room. I wasn't even the fifth most in shape. I assumed a headstand had to do with physical ability, but my experience at the ashram was showing me, over and over, that what I know isn't always the case.

Sophie tried again. And, after a bit of patient guidance from the yogi, she pushed through. Without the assistance of the wall, she popped up into a headstand. I could see her smile, upside down.

It's obvious. Our preconceived notions can control us.

I get it.

Sophie came down from her headstand with a beaming smile still on her face. The yogi managed to crack a smile, too, just enough for her to see the method in his instruction.

Later, the teacher shared so many insightful things about the ego: what it is, why it's harmful, how we can take steps to control it. Everything I thought I knew about ego was wrong. Mind you, that wasn't much.

Molly and I both furiously took notes. That afternoon, we exchanged thoughts about how our lives were and how we'd like some aspects of them to be. In such a short time at the ashram, my mind had been opened to exploring how those shifts could positively impact my life.

DAY THREE

At morning meditation, something very different happened, something I don't think I could have expected or even perhaps *should* have expected. Somehow, as the chanting washed over me, I surrendered to it on a level deeper than I knew was possible. What unfolded was unlike anything I had experienced before, and I can only describe it as transcendent. It left me with an unshakable sense that we all have a purpose in life, and mine was clear to me.

At lunch, I was so happy to see the swami, the ashram's spiritual leader, eating by himself. I approached him with my tray of food. "May I join you?" I asked.

"Of course," he said.

To have an opportunity to speak one-on-one with him was a special thing. If I had gone at a different time of year, when the ashram was busier, it likely wouldn't have happened.

"I wonder if I could tell you about something that happened to me this morning during meditation," I said. "Do you mind if I tell you while you eat?"

He invited me to share.

I explained my lack of experience and also told him about what happened during my meditation, in great detail. I asked him if that was what meditation was supposed to feel like, because that morning, it felt as though something was really happening.

"My friend," he said. "You had a very rare experience, one that few people have in a lifetime. It was probably your naivete and lack of preconceived expectations that allowed you to experience what you did. You must never share the details of your experience with anyone. If you do, it will further their preconceived expectations of what meditation should be. Then they will always be looking for an experience like the one you had, rather than experiencing their own."

An experience very few have in a lifetime?

While meditating, I had no idea what was happening, and now I was overwhelmed, wondering why and how this had happened for me.

Regardless, I was acutely aware that I would never be the same again. This trip, this place, it was proving to be powerful, almost beyond me.

DAY FOUR

This day, the schedule of the retreat felt like second nature. I was comfortable. I had made friends. I felt nourished in my body, mind, and soul. I had learned more than I thought I ever would. A part of me didn't want to leave.

Before we broke for bed, the swami invited us to meet the next day at the beach for a meditation at six in the morning. He didn't tell us why, but assuming that it would be like the other experiences I'd garnered during the retreat, I looked forward to waking up and finding out.

DAY FIVE

We met at the beach, ten of us, in the darkness of the morning. We were told the experience was going to follow the pattern of what we had done in the temple, except we would begin with a silent walk and then we would greet the day as the sun rose, while we meditated.

We walked barefoot in silence. There was nobody else on the beach at that very early hour.

The swami led us along the high-tide line. Some yogis walked with us. Sophie and Taryn were behind Molly and me. The waves rolled in gently, up to our footprints.

Ours were the first set of tracks on the beach.

I stepped in others' footprints, crisscrossing them as we walked.

Here, among all these footprints, were also mine.

As I noticed all the footprints, I couldn't help but think: *We all have a destination.* We want to be fulfilled in some way, shape, or form: in family, in work, in love. We all want to be fulfilled, but the path to fulfillment is different for everyone. So many of us are living with other people's intentions as our goal. We impose our expectations on others. Parents do this to their children. We do it to our friends, our coworkers, and our employees. We do it to our significant others. I'd always done what was expected of me—working hard, making more money, and attaining greater heights of success—but at times it crushed my soul, and I lost myself by following the footsteps of others.

We stopped walking, faced the sunrise, and greeted the day.

We sat in the sand.

We met the sun and chanted.

I still didn't know the words, but the melodies were locked in, and I hummed along as the sun kissed my face. I noticed now the space in my mind. I realized that I could meditate. I could control my thoughts. I could create a vast, open space in this busy, cluttered mind when I wanted to. When I needed to. When I chose to.

Later that day, I said my goodbyes to the three new friends I had made. I knew our bond would forever connect us, especially me and Molly, who was beside me throughout the retreat, at every turn.

But they aren't the only people I met at the ashram over those five days.

I met a new me. I met myself.

10

EGO

TAPPING INTO GRACE

THE CODI who booked the yoga trip was not the same Codi who came home.

I don't mean to suggest that my trip to the ashram righted all the courses of my life, but it sure made me aware of what's important and how to behave when life gets too cluttered and overwhelming. I also learned how to adjust my path so I can get to the place where I want, or even need, to be.

I learned how to identify and control my ego.

Before I went to the ashram, I had always defined "ego" in the context of an arrogant person: "Oh, that person is an egomaniac," or "That person has a huge ego."

But ego, I learned, is something everyone has.

Ego is the omnipresent voice in your head that questions you.

It questions your limits.

It questions your courage.

It questions your abilities and skills and relationships. It questions everything.

Too often, it tells you that you're not good enough.

The ego is rarely positive or encouraging. On the contrary, your ego often counters your positive thoughts. If you say, "I can do this!" your ego says, "Are you sure about that?" But when you say, "I'm not good enough," it agrees with you.

All those negative thoughts that fill your head are coming from your ego.

I want you to understand your ego's power and its ability to influence you. Because when you realize what ego is, you can control it and find a freedom you've never known before.

Your ego always tries to control the conversations that you have with yourself, which is why you have to learn to recognize its voice. So you know when it's trying to take over.

When you see your ego for what it is, you can keep it at arm's length. But when it's active and you aren't aware? Your ego can wreak havoc in your life, especially in your relationships.

A quote from the sage Lao-tzu says:

> When I let go of what I am, I become what I might be. When I let go of what I have, I receive what I need.

If you replace the "what I am" and "what I have" with "my ego," look what happens:

> When I let go of my ego, I become what I might be. When I let go of my ego, I receive what I need.

When you let go of who you think you are, you meet your awakened true self.

But here's the challenge: Ego is so damn smart and so damn strong. It constantly collects experiences that bolster its strength inside you, like a hurricane gaining strength from the warm Atlantic waters to unleash its fury on land. Your experiences are that warm water.

The past is one of our greatest influencers. What has happened to us is a great predictor of how we will conduct ourselves going forward.

If you've been burned by love three times, how likely is it that you'll want to fall in love again? Even if, at your core, your true self hungers for compassion and partnership, your ego will tell you that everything about love is bad. It will list every single reason you should never allow yourself to love again.

And your past isn't just about you. Others have influenced your past and continue to affect your ego greatly. Egos love the company of others like them because egos are mutual enablers.

You've heard the saying, "Misery loves company." Miserable egos love the company of other gloomy egos because they give one another power. Their mutual negativity flames the fires of despair.

But an amazing thing happens when we learn about controlling our ego. If we're around a negative person, we start to be able to see that buried within them is a beautiful soul, but their ego is so loudly pronounced in their life that it commands their actions.

When you can understand that a person may be acting under the compulsion of their ego, you can walk away from a negative experience and say, "Okay, that was a miserable ego," rather than, "Wow, what a miserable person!"

If you believe that we all have a higher purpose—a greater, deeper truth inside ourselves—you will distinguish between a person's ego and who they truly are.

To some of you, this may all sound like hocus-pocus. You might be thinking, *All this talk about ego isn't important. Let's skip to the next chapter.* Enter Exhibit A: that's your ego talking. It doesn't want you to recognize it, because then it will lose its power.

I get it. It was only when I saw how the ego was pushing me around the hustle that I understood the truth about this. All the success I had wasn't mine. It was the success of my ego, which constantly told me I had to work harder, do more, be the best.

When I recognized that, I had a moment of awakening.

My success was not a reflection of my authentic self. My ego had been fueling my purpose and passion, driving me. Sometimes the ego is so powerful that it consumes us and distracts us from what we truly desire. It buries our authentic self so deeply that the ego is assured of its control. That was my experience.

But the more we align with our true selves and buck the messages of the ego, the more we take away its strength and power.

Remember the story about Sophie and her headstand? Her ego was in full play that day, telling her she couldn't do it, that she wasn't strong enough to manage that difficult pose. It made her angry and frustrated. But when the teacher insisted that her ego was wrong, Sophie persisted, and we all learned a lesson about how to identify the ego.

Maybe you see yourself in Sophie's story, or mine. Maybe your story is not about the hustle or yoga but about another aspect of life where you recognize your ego at play.

The ego can get so heavy that it tips the scale and sets off alerts, letting us know when it's gaining traction. When my ego is really active and loud, I find myself questioning my thoughts. So when I hear that undermining voice, I've trained myself to stop and ask, *Who is that?* I ask why I would be thinking about something this way or judging myself or someone else so harshly.

Maybe not everyone's ego is quite that strong, but I suspect that at some point, for everyone, the ego is stronger than we would like to admit and perhaps is in control more than we would like it to be.

Ego can show up in a variety of ways. It might equate things such as money and status with success, comparing you with your friends and colleagues to see how you stack up. It might stop you from trying things. It may undermine your ability to do something you're fully capable of doing, as in Sophie's example.

What are the examples from your own life? If you pause for a minute and consider the times your ego has shown up, I'm confident you'll think of something, even if you're not proud to admit what that something is.

Maybe, as it did with me and my father, your ego shows up in your relationships. My ego told me that Bob should have been a better father, a better man. That he should have had a meaningful presence in his son's life, that I deserved a proper dad. Yes, I did deserve those things, and yet there were more profound truths living beyond my ego's construct. When I got some distance from that wall of my ego, I could see beyond it and realize that, yes, those things were important, but it was biology that made Bob a father, and me his son.

Just because you have a child doesn't mean, by default, that you'll be a good parent. And being a lousy parent doesn't strip you of all the other good things you can be.

Bob wasn't a great father, but he was a great friend and had attributes that contributed to others' lives in a meaningful way. Had death not interrupted us, he and I might have found a friendship that wasn't possible in our father–son dynamic. To reconcile any fractured relationship, you need to control your ego. Sometimes, when you get started in your work with ego, you come to understand that, so often, there's more than meets the eye.

It doesn't mean just blindly accepting that there's good in everyone. And don't expect to like and get along with every person in your life. The point is that, with some objectivity, there's usually more to see and understand, there are other truths in the story. Controlling your ego means committing to seeing life from that perspective. That alone is incredibly liberating. Giving more energy to the belief that there are other sides to the story than you might get at face value is so much better than continually struggling to reconcile someone's behavior or intent.

Controlling the ego means having the perspective to say, "There's more here than I know or am being told." My ego went to Bob's funeral thinking he didn't even deserve one. But at the funeral, I kept my mind opened wide enough to think, *Okay. Here's more information. Here's a perspective I didn't have before. Wow. His friends really loved him.* When I let that point of view sit, and I stopped justifying all the ego's comments inside my head, I saw something I hadn't noticed before. When I focused on that new discovery, I started to understand more about who Bob really was. Who that was, was someone I could admire, and that wasn't an emotion I had ever experienced where he was concerned.

Most people probably have relationships in their life that are difficult. Perhaps you're wrestling with something similar in your own life. That tug-of-war is the ego and your sense of perspective struggling to strike a balance. Pay attention and you'll hear an inner voice that's trying to rise above the strife. That's your true self countering the ego.

Controlling the ego can be a constant struggle. You might think, *I should try to be nicer. I should try to be more patient. I should try harder.* And so you adjust your behavior. But the next day you're back to thinking, *Ugh. I hate being around those people. They really bother me.* Then another voice pipes up: *I don't know what's going on in their world. I should be kinder.* Then, the next day, they drive you up the wall again. Rest assured, however, that if you experience this type of struggle, you're already trying to get control over your ego.

If I had allowed my ego to continue controlling the conversation, I would never have found a way to make peace with Bob, and what a shame that would have been. Our relationship is irreparable, because he is dead. I had to come to terms with things on my own. I could have chosen to keep feeling slighted, but I decided to look at the relationship through another lens. Through grace.

Grace is powerful. Grace is different from forgiveness. You may have heard someone say, "I will forgive, but I won't forget." The truth is, it's hard to forget things that hurt us. Our brains don't have an erase button. We have repositories of beautiful memories we hold on to; we can hear the voices of loved ones who are no longer with us; we can reimagine experiences that we never want to forget. Aromas we recall can bring us joy. The remarkable capacity to recall happy memories makes us appreciate the brain for the splendid organ that it is. And yet the flip side of this is that we have the same ability to recall the bad things. For all the pleasing things the brain retains, it holds on to unfavorable memories, too.

So it's true: we don't forget. But we can spin a negative memory into something far more positive. This is grace.

When you let empathy play a significant role in situations that are out of your control, that is grace. Grace is liberating. It is for me.

In my role as a funeral director, I once sat with a family who chose to extend grace to someone who had taken the life of their loved one. It was a powerful thing to witness. Most people couldn't fathom how they were able to grant such kindness. I remember being touched by how profound it was for them to offer this grace. And in imparting it, they liberated themselves from the chains of something they couldn't change and took control of the narrative going forward.

This family showed me the power of grace. And surely, if they could find it in their situation, I can employ some grace in my own life, every single day.

We can't find grace until we learn to control the ego. Ego is humanity's greatest addiction, and the world would be a far better place if we all attended "Egos Anonymous."

When you can identify ego, you see that when you're having a bad day and you're really dwelling on it, your ego has taken control. You see the same in others, and you know that this doesn't make them bad, negative humans, it just means their egos are in charge.

But empathy can build its strength and resolve the same way the ego does. Giving your power to empathy and perspective instead of ego is an excellent placement of energy.

I'll give you an example.

Let's imagine you're running late and you're on the way to the bank. You see someone backing out of a parking spot, and you put your turn signal on and wait patiently for them to leave. Then, someone pulls in and takes the spot. You have a choice: You can grumble and complain and let it ruin your morning. Or you can simply say to yourself, *That person needed the spot more than I did. I don't know what's going on in their life and I'm not entitled to know, but in my grace, from one human to another, their purpose put them ahead of me to take that spot.*

And leave it at that.

Most times, we race to anger and judgment, abandoning any semblance of control as we hurl negativity toward the person behind the wheel.

The part of you that wants to wallow in annoyance is your ego. But if we silence it for a moment, we may realize: *My day is no more important than their day.* Maybe that person is on their way to an appointment at the hospital, and they're picking up urgent documents. Perhaps their loved one just received a life-threatening diagnosis, and they're distracted and disoriented right now. If you take a moment to conjure the extreme in situations like this, the result can be calming and very powerful.

When we treat humanity in general with more conscious kindness, the Universe responds.

This all contributes to living your Everyday Legacy.

11

WHERE YOU MEET YOURSELF

DISCOVERING THE REAL YOU

WHEN I returned from the ashram and to my daily routines, surrounded by the same people I had been a mere five days before, I realized something was different: me. I found that I was more attracted to myself. I was more interesting, more flexible. Not as rigid.

My entire corporate career had forced me to be adaptable. Or so I thought.

I could pack a bag and be out the door, on the way to the airport, in under ten minutes. I could sit through twenty meetings in a day. I thought I was adaptable, but I was just a Ping-Pong ball bouncing back and forth on the same table, time after time. I didn't consider that I might have a depth beneath all that. I simply wasn't aware.

One aspect of the beauty of going beyond your comfort zone is finding the parts of yourself that have been hidden away from your awareness. My brain was quick enough to know that I needed a push. Somewhere inside, I knew that another version of Codi was buried beneath my ego. Something urged me to go looking for him, and that meant taking some time just for me.

Many of us have been programmed to believe that putting ourselves first and doing things for ourselves ahead of others is selfish. Most of us are raised to be selfless. Most of us are taught that it is better to give than to receive.

But I submit that we must put ourselves first if we are going to be of service to others. This is what I call being "self-full."

Being self-full is an investment in you and your connection with yourself. It's a space that allows you to realize that to help others, to show up in others' lives, to affect others in a meaningful way, the first step is to meet yourself.

I was in the audience of an Oprah Lifeclass once, right in the front row while she interviewed inspirational speaker and television personality Iyanla Vanzant about this very topic.

Two things about that conversation stood out for me. One is that the way you treat yourself is the way you treat God (or whatever you call that higher, guiding force). If you put yourself last, you're putting God last. You have to be as good to yourself as you would be to God. The second is that you have to fill up your own cup if you're going to be of service to others. Whatever overflows from the cup is for everyone else, but what's in the cup is yours. If your cup isn't overflowing, you have nothing to give, and if your cup isn't full, it can't overflow.

As I learned to become present, I saw that this alternate version of me wasn't beyond myself, but was *within* myself. In short, I found myself by being present and by being self-full.

I pulled myself away from what I knew with the intention of finding a new me. Of course, there was no "new me" to discover. The me I was seeking was always there, but I had never taken the time to stop and look for him. To do that, I had to clear my mind of all the clutter I'd accumulated over the years, through some pretty deep introspection.

We all have it—mental junk we gather as kids and young adults, notions about how to live that are based on other people's expectations. Think of children who are told they'll grow up to be scientists, so they force themselves to pursue a degree in biology even though they want a career in the arts. Or the children who dream of being artists, but they're led to believe they can't make a living that way, so they give up on themselves before they even give their dream a chance.

We've all grown up with thoughts that cause us to lose bits of ourselves. I was living with an illusion of how the world should work. I had ideas of what I considered to be accomplishments or success, all deriving from other people. I believed I had to work harder than anyone else and earn more money than anyone else, as though I were in a race to a finish line that didn't exist. None of that mind-clutter served me, but it wasn't until I paused and experienced being present that I realized that what was driving me didn't make sense.

Being present allowed me to unload a lot of mental clutter so I could finally see Codi again, and I saw that I was enough, just as I was.

And so, the experience of returning home to my regular life was jarring, plunked as I was back into reality, no longer on a beach in the Bahamas practicing yoga and meditation every day with all those like-minded people. As much as I would have loved to sell everything, run away to a tropical island,

and become a yoga master, I had bills to pay. Real life makes it tough to manage that sort of departure.

But, because I took the time to pause at the ashram, I now had a point of reference to return to when I felt overwhelmed by life. I know what it means to be present. I know how it feels and how to get there, and I make sure that I take breaks and reflect. A lot of the time, people read books or go to conferences and feel inspired, but I was fortunate enough to experience more than a momentary inspiration. That retreat sparked an aspiration in me to go through life as a better version of myself. It gave me the motivation to live with more presence.

I hope that, as you read this book, you'll see yourself in these pages and also feel this sort of aspiration. I hope you're feeling inspired to be present more often, whether that means learning to meditate or minding your own thoughts every morning while you brush your teeth. Try to stop doing ten things at once. Take a breath. Just one, and then another after that. Calm, simple breaths.

When you feel what it is to be present, as tough as it can be to get there, you will find your way back.

Sometimes, all it takes is a tiny shift in the way you look at something.

A small shift in perspective.

We're so used to seeing things one way that we might feel it's impossible to see things otherwise. But then you make a tiny shift—and just like that, your view changes, and you might not ever be able to look at life the old way again.

Take this line of letters:

OPPORTUNITYISNOWHERE

You can read that as either "opportunity is nowhere" or "opportunity is now here." A small shift in how you choose to see the words completely changes the meaning.

Being present is a very complex idea. You might think of it as quite simple, and yet it's not easy to achieve. It is not only a destination. It's an experience.

Being present is where you meet yourself.

We meet ourselves when we are in our element, living our truth and practicing our greatness. When writers are lost in their words, they are meeting themselves. In their element, builders saw and hammer only to discover they've built a beautiful piece of furniture out of sheer passion. Drama teachers tirelessly and passionately put energy into their students, and so they create a superb production. Musicians compose a symphony from a place of expansiveness where they meet themselves.

When you become so lost in what you are creating that everything is a blur until you finish, and in the end you make a masterpiece, that is a good sign that you are in your truth and you have met yourself.

Whatever your masterpiece is, you can find endless amounts of energy in the act of producing it. Even if you are exhausted, you can push through, as though you were doing something beyond yourself. In fact, this is where you meet yourself.

In that moment when nothing seems to matter except what you're doing, you're meeting yourself. When what you're doing is all that matters, you have met your truest self. It's usually not in life's hectic moments that this happens, but in the quiet ones.

When your heart swells, and your consciousness is alert, those are good indicators that you're present.

Sometimes, the destination is as important as the journey. In this case, being present is both the trip and your arrival.

Discovering what it meant to be present scared me, because the experience confused me. I had no idea such a sensation of peace could exist within myself.

I had nothing to compare it to, because I had never quieted my mind before. I'd never meditated. No previous experience in my life had prepared me for it. But learning how to be present gave me a landing place. A place to return to when I find myself caught up in the hustle.

Someone once said that people come into our lives for a reason, a season, or a lifetime. I would add "fleeting moment" to that list, in the context of the Codi I began to meet regularly when I returned from the ashram. Before that time, he had made only the briefest of appearances; the hustle had scared him off, undoubtedly. That Codi could easily have been someone I met only for fleeting moments now and then. But after a mere five days, almost unbelievably, this version of Codi turned out to be someone I knew could stick around for a lifetime, if only I invited him in and created the space for him to stay.

12

FINGER SNAP PEOPLE

A COMMUNITY OF KINDNESS

WHEN I was a kid, I had my own business. At the young age of fourteen, before it was legal to work in a typical business setting, I was a salesperson for a national direct selling company that was quite popular in rural communities, where there were few to no department stores.

I sold wrapping paper and greeting cards, housewares and gift items. No, it wasn't common to see a young teenager acting as a sales representative for this particular company, but I believe I've already established that I wasn't exactly a "normal" kid.

I'd hop on my BMX bicycle and head off to my neighbors' houses, dropping off catalogs, taking orders, and delivering packages. I sat with them and drank tea and visited until my mother called around to see if anyone knew where Codi was, and could you please ask him to come home for dinner?

Besides this business of mine, I was involved in tons of other activities. I'd tried playing guitar, karate, swimming... You name it and I tried it, but I couldn't seem to find a place where I fit in.

In later years, after postsecondary school, as I began to climb the corporate ladder, I accelerated very quickly. At twenty-three years old, I was the youngest person ever to reach a management position in my company. My counterparts were all older than me—many, significantly so.

I learned very quickly that management is a lonely place, especially when your peers have twenty years on you. I didn't fit there, either.

It wasn't until I met myself in the Bahamas that I started to attract the people I wanted to be surrounded by.

You could say that I didn't know what community meant, until I knew.

Motivational speaker Jim Rohn is widely quoted as having said, "You are the average of the five people you spend the most time with," suggesting that these five people ultimately shape who you are.

The more kindness you have in your life, the more people you attract who appreciate kindness. The more peace you have in your life, the more peace you attract. The more you infuse your life with joy, the more joyous people are drawn to you. The opposite of these positives is also true: if you surround yourself with negative people, then negativity can become your average, too.

I didn't know I was craving deep connections with like-minded and like-valued people until I found myself surrounded by them.

One evening in June 2018, I invited a group of eleven people to dinner to discuss Everyday Legacy. These weren't just any people; I considered those sitting around the table to be my go-to people. These were not just friends, but trusted people in my life who had been placed in my path for some reason. I invited this group not only because I love these people, but also because I genuinely value their instinct and intellect.

I wanted to share my vision for this book with them. This was my tribe. These were my people. And when I looked around the table at the faces of those who had come out to support me in this adventure, I realized that some of them were people I'd known only for a few months. Some, I'd only spent a couple of hours with in person. But with all of them, the moment I met them, I felt instant attraction—pure magnetism.

I've started calling these people my "finger snap people," because that's how long it takes to know that I've found them: the duration of the snap of a finger. Our energy is almost palpable, and I just want to be in their company. It's like a match striking the matchbox.

They are my community.

Maybe a higher power had steered me away from other groups in the past. Or perhaps I was a member of certain tribes before, but there was so little in the way of connection for me that I didn't recognize them as such. Perhaps, before I knew how to control my ego, it had driven me to squeeze into places where I didn't fit. But not anymore. Now I know where I belong and who I should align myself with.

When it's hard to articulate why you are attracted to someone, that's often a sign that it's a good fit. If you can't quite figure out if it's a characteristic or value they possess, or a feeling they give you, then learning more about them is likely worth exploring. Sometimes when it's inexplicable, that explains it all. Perhaps you admire a combination of their qualities, such as passion, loyalty, conviction, and honesty.

There's so much noise about who we should be and how we should show up in the world, how much money we should make and whether we should rent a place to live or buy a home, and what kind of car we should drive; all these are ego-driven directives that can propel us toward things we shouldn't gravitate to. We're living in a bit of a fictitious world now, where everything is stylized. Posts on social media wipe all of the beautiful imperfections away.

Don't we all intuitively know it's better to be real? In a job interview, be as honest, raw, and authentic as you possibly can. If you play a role during an interview and the employer likes what they see, and they hire you, you face pretending to be someone you're not for as long as you have that job. That won't work. It will make you miserable. And your employer will have hired a different person than they thought they were getting.

With all the noise out there, if you show up in the world in a way that's inauthentic, it's almost impossible to be heard for who you truly are. Most people can't cut through the noise to perceive that.

The more we're in alignment with ourselves and our values, the more we live and breathe our true Everyday Legacy. The more we express what our values mean to us, how they impact our life and change who and how we are in the world, the more we'll be surrounded by others who have been traveling similar roads.

When we show up as our most authentic selves, that alone attracts the right people to us.

Life puts people in front of us, but it's up to us to notice them and to act. Once we're aware that one of these people is standing before us, we need to act. We can't rely on the Universe to just put these people there and then take care of everything else as well. That's like putting a check in front of someone who never takes it to the bank. It's just paper with words and numbers until we do something with it.

CREATE YOUR COMMUNITY

Are you surrounded by people who support, invigorate, ignite, and inspire you? Do the people in your life compel you to show up more honestly, lovingly, or empathetically?

Whatever Everyday Legacy means to you, if you have a community that motivates you to show up with more authenticity, more frequently, then you're with the right people. If not, they're out there somewhere. You just have to pay attention to the clues leading you to them.

Community is powerful. It's like building a sports team and picking the players from a worldwide roster, choosing who you want on your team. Who do you wish to strategize with to bring home the first-place trophy?

When a team achieves victory and celebrates the big win, after the flashes of the cameras and the videos and the interviews, when the arena goes quiet, I don't expect that team cares all that much about the cup itself. What they care about are the people they won it with. Everything else falls away, and you're left with lessons, memories, and connections that leave you with an almost inexplicable feeling of camaraderie. That's community.

When you're in alignment with yourself, and you're living your Everyday Legacy, community will sustain you. It's like the oxygen you need to live. You take a breath of air like you've never taken before.

When you're in congruence with your Everyday Legacy and keeping true to the values that are important to you, you become a magnet. The more you attract people who share your values, the stronger the magnetic pull. The Universe mobilizes you until you get to where you're supposed to be.

It's important to have a group of people you can lean on, to have someone there when you need empathy, someone you can be there for, too.

My community is a source of support and accountability for me, and whenever someone needs something, I'm there for them. It's a symbiotic relationship. Whether it's your personal or your professional life, without the right people around you, it's a little duller.

Consider the activities you love to do and the people with whom you love doing them. What do these activities and people add to your life?

Even if you love doing absolutely nothing with someone, that's still doing something. The only time you're truly doing nothing is when you're dead. Even then, your legacy lives beyond you, just as my grandmother's legacy does at teatime, when I turn on the kettle.

I mentioned earlier that we are the by-products of the five people we spend the most time with.

Sit with that for a moment...

Who shows up most in your life? Who most frequently occupies your time and energy?

Sometimes, until we take time to think about it, we are unaware of who's in our circle of five. And then the realization can be debilitating. What if our five people aren't creating the kind of value we need to draw out our better selves? What if we're married to someone like that? Perhaps your spouse has lost their joie de vivre, and you're just hitting your stride. What then? Or maybe an immediate family member is negative all the time, and cutting them out of your life isn't entirely possible. How do you manage that?

In an ideal world, we would seek out and choose five people who elevate us to new heights and bring out our best. But in the real world, it is often people we wouldn't choose for our circle who are around us the most—a parent, sibling, child, or colleague. We may necessarily spend a large portion of our energy and time on those relationships, and that can make us feel infringed upon. While it may be that certain people you're around a lot wouldn't be among the five you'd choose for yourself, you can still gain a powerful advantage from these relationships. Just as powerful, in fact, as if you had chosen them.

If your child isn't as ambitious as you would like someone in your circle of five to be? Use their lack of ambition to fuel your ambition to be a loving parent. When you catch yourself focusing on what bothers you about your child, use it as a reminder to funnel your energy into telling them what they do that makes you proud.

Let's say a parent you have to care for is perpetually negative, always in a space of doom and gloom. Draw strength from that. Let that negativity remind you to look for the silver lining in situations.

So, when we talk about our circle of five, it's not about eradicating from it the people who don't meet certain criteria. It's about being purposeful in our intent with those people.

Every person who enters our life does so for a reason. Sometimes we're not aware of what the reason is until after they leave. This applies to those who play major roles in our lives; those who drift in, out, and back in again; and those who make cameo appearances, such as the person ahead of us in a line who was rude to the cashier. When it's our turn, we can decide how to interact with that employee. We can either display awareness or we can display humanity.

Awareness might manifest itself in a comment on the rude person's behavior. But that's not doing any more than stating the obvious. It's just verbalizing what you saw.

Humanity is engaging with others in a positive way, letting our actions speak louder than our words. Instead of commiserating with the cashier about how nasty that customer was, we could look them in the eye and say, "You handle jerks like a pro! Have any tips for me?"

That will likely elicit a smile and a conversation, and chances are that we've changed the course of where that person's day was headed. This is the stuff that makes a difference in people's lives.

We don't have to make grand gestures. The most meaningful moments can happen in the simplest of ways.

When like-minded individuals with common, positive values come together, they start to mobilize humanity, because a group of focused people who are directed toward the same goal is more powerful than one person trying to achieve something on their own.

Creating a community that evolves and grows, where people constantly push each other positively, starts with you.

One of the best pieces of business advice I've ever received came from a mentor who said, "Ask yourself: when you look back on your forty-year career, do you want to have one year repeated forty times, or forty individual years filled with new and insightful ideas, growth, and successes?" Likewise, I encourage you to create a story so bright and varied that, when you look back on it at the end of your life, it will be hard to pinpoint all the many ways you positively influenced people.

That is a life of legacy.

13

SHOULDER TAPS

BEING LAZY TO TUNE IN

FOR MANY Indigenous peoples, the sound of drums is said to symbolize Earth's beating heart, connecting the drummer's spirit to that of the Great Spirit.

In the Hindu religion, "om" is a sacred spiritual sound made during prayer or meditation, and during important ceremonies. Om refers to the human soul and the Supreme Spirit, the Divine, the Universe.

Christians recite prayers and join together to sing hymns to God.

The vocabulary and the rituals are different, but the purpose is the same: a connection to something greater.

Our humanity is simply the vehicle carrying us through our spiritual journey toward whatever is waiting for us at the other end. As the French Jesuit priest Pierre Teilhard de Chardin is famously quoted as saying: "We are not human beings having a spiritual experience. We are spiritual beings having a human experience."

For as long as I can remember, something inside me has stirred. Before I decided to write this book, I couldn't have told you what that stirring was. I just felt an overwhelming sense that I had a greater purpose; that I was being prepared for something.

I had tried more than once to write books about business, and the successful strategies I'd gathered and implemented over the years. My attempts flopped. I usually couldn't get past the first chapter, and even that was often terrible. But the moment I made up my mind to write *Everyday Legacy*, something shifted. I started to type and couldn't stop. I would often have to stop typing and start talking out loud, recording my thoughts and transcribing them later because my fingers couldn't keep up.

Then I began to tell people what I was writing about, and they were interested. They wanted to know more. As I dialed into the energy of the Universe, that stirring I'd felt became a longing, and I started to notice things happening: moments when alignment became more apparent, so much so that I couldn't help but pay attention to it. I call these "shoulder taps."

You've probably experienced shoulder taps, too. Such as when you're thinking of someone and they call you. Or when an old song you were just talking about comes on the radio. Or when you've started a new endeavor and you happen to meet someone who has expertise that can help you. The Universe is gently tapping on your shoulder, saying, "Hey, you. Pay attention. Pay attention to what you're hearing/seeing/feeling right now."

Some people describe this as God whispering in their ear. Others might say it's a creepy coincidence. It doesn't matter what you call these moments. What matters is that you pay attention to them. That you acknowledge their power. Because when these things happen, something bigger is calling out to you.

We're moving so fast that we easily miss the nuances. We don't pick up on people's feelings. We brush past things that need our attention. We miss the shoulder taps.

Imagine someone standing behind you, waiting to get your attention while your head is down at your computer, or you're scrolling through your newsfeed or daydreaming about one of the million things you have to do. Maybe that person whispers something important to you, but you're too distracted to notice.

The more time you take to pause in your day, the more likely you'll be to notice those shoulder taps. And the more you notice and acknowledge them, the more they'll happen. When the Universe sees that you're paying attention and moving toward something, it propels you further in the right direction.

I was at a dinner with some other entrepreneurs, around the time I started writing this book. Throughout the evening, we'd taken turns talking about our businesses, and I had shared the concept of Everyday Legacy with the people around the table. It was the first time I'd spoken about it to a group, and the concept captured their attention.

One of the dinner guests had created a set of cards with questions on them, intended to inspire deep, meaningful conversations. Usually, the facilitator of the event would pose questions to spark discussion; but on this particular evening, we decided to use the cards to lead the conversation.

We were each invited to draw a card from the deck and answer the question written on it. At my turn, I reached into the deck, selected a card, and read it silently to myself. I couldn't help but smile as I did.

It read, *How do you want to be remembered?*

Everyone around the table admitted to having goosebumps.

I took the card as a clear message from the Universe: writing this book was exactly what I needed to do. I had been given more than a shoulder tap; the universe nudged, almost shoved, me.

Shoulder taps affirm that something can be created in our life. A higher power puts us in touch with the right tools or people, and if we're willing to put in the work, astonishing things can happen. But we have to pay conscious attention and pick up when the Universe calls. Otherwise, there comes a point when the Universe tires of trying to reach us. When we're too distracted to notice the shoulder taps, they stop happening.

What we're working toward should make us come alive. If you feel you're being pushed toward something other than your most authentic self, that's not what you're after. But, as the old Scottish phrase says, "Whit's fer ye'll no go by ye!"—what's meant for you won't pass you by.

As you find yourself moving closer to alignment, you'll probably hear from your ego. And you'll know it when it shows up. Remember, it's the voice that says awful things to you. Things like, "You're not good enough. Nobody's going to like that. Give it up!" Once you know what it sounds like, you can learn not to give in to the ego. The best way to disarm it is to focus on the shoulder taps until they are louder than it is.

Then you're on your way to freedom.

Think of shoulder taps as the heartbeat of your authenticity, as the drumbeat channeling the spirit of the Universe through you. Or you might imagine the taps as a metronome, keeping you on pace.

When you focus on the steady, rhythmic beating of these taps from a higher power, you suddenly have a cadence. A purpose. A reminder to keep going, keep moving, stay on pace. When your ego flares, tune in to the beat, and that sound will get louder again.

Creating the space to pause for alignment is like winding the metronome. When I started to write this book, even though the shoulder taps were coming fast and furious, I was letting life lead me around. I decided I had to consciously carve out the time to write or the book would never happen. So I blocked off my schedule on Wednesdays for working on it. On Wednesdays, I wound up the metronome to set my cadence for the week. Throughout the week, I could still hear the ticking, but by the following Wednesday the metronome needing winding again.

Shoulder taps are the Universe telling you something. It won't say exactly what you should do, but your heart and mind will work together to guide you along the right path. The Universe may steer you in the right direction, but your destiny is a two-way street.

The Universe requires some reciprocity for you to manifest more of what you want in your life. It's not all hocus-pocus; it does take some work. You could sit around and think about being a millionaire all day long, but until you positively work toward that goal, it's not going to happen. (Well ... unless you inherit a fortune or win a lottery.) The more work you put in, the more taps you'll receive, until the taps feel more like a nudge. That is a sign that you're coming into alignment.

Alignment is your higher purpose. Your greater calling. Your most authentic self. When you experience more taps, you won't be able to deny that you're on the right path: Here's more proof. Here's another person to help you on your way. Another tool or idea that will help you manifest your heart's desire.

This will enable you to reveal more of yourself and to share your genius with the world.

BE LAZY

The best way to experience more shoulder taps is by being lazy.

That's right: *be lazy*.

For a lot of people, the word "lazy" has a negative connotation. As children, we're told not to be lazy. Get off your butt. Do something.

In high school, if we get poor grades, we must have been lazy.

In university, we're told that if we're lazy, we won't succeed.

In our careers, being lazy usually gets us nowhere.

When people come to me looking for clarity in situations where they can't seem to find any, I tell them to be lazy with it and see what happens.

Telling people to be lazy as if it is a positive thing raises eyebrows. How can being lazy be a good thing?

I get it.

For so many years, I was the antithesis of lazy. I didn't stop. I put my pedal to the floor and barely let up. My career was my life. I was attached to my phone until I went to bed, and then again the moment I opened my eyes in the morning.

Near the end of my corporate career, I was entitled to six weeks of vacation a year and I often took only two. Not for lack of wanting a holiday, but my schedule was so packed that I rarely stopped to realize I needed downtime.

When I did, I just crashed. I needed to shut down physically to recharge.

To be lazy was the opposite of everything I knew. So, when I left my corporate career and went out on my own, I was in for a shock.

Overnight, I went from earning a six-figure salary and driving a company car to having no paycheck, no car, no perks. It all disappeared as quickly as flipping a switch.

It's not as though I had worked like a dog and hated my life—my ego loved it. But when I shifted gears, I wound up in a completely different world: same Codi, entirely changed circumstances.

In this new world, I had time to think. Not about where I was going next or what plane I had to catch or who I was meeting with or what group I was presenting to. I could think about whatever I wanted. For the first time in so many years, I had room to breathe.

It was a real adjustment to become comfortable with gaps in my schedule and spans of time without commitments. I felt lazy.

It became a catchphrase among my friends that I'd had a lazy day, which meant I had time to think and contemplate.

To plan and prepare. In being lazy, I got clear. I slowed down enough to see the type of work I was most passionate about and fueled by, and the kind that drained me.

Before I left the corporate world, I had been that person who couldn't hear the Universe whispering right behind me. I was so distracted by all the things that seemed important: the phone calls, the text messages, the social media notifications, the e-mails. The hustle manifested lots of good in my life, but being lazy helped me to not get lost in it.

There's a space that can fuel even more success and happiness, more alignment with your truer self. For me, that space was lazy. My lazy space became productive. I found the beauty in a place that I had, for so long, been programmed to believe was negative. For my entire life, I had believed being lazy had no value. When I was a kid, all my report cards came back with the same comments:

"Codi talks too much."
"Codi is very distracted in class."
"Codi doesn't pay attention."

My parents would say, "Codi, pay attention in class and stop talking so much." And so I kept trying to talk less in class and to be less distracted.

During that lazy time after I ended my corporate career, I contemplated how these qualities might be some of my greatest strengths. I love talking, and I wanted to do more of it. In fact, I wanted to earn a living doing the very thing the teachers complained about.

As for that distracted state my teachers pointed out? That "distraction" is a busy mind. It's me looking for different angles, solutions, and perspectives. One might call that being innovative.

In this time of being lazy, I began to notice the shoulder taps. "Lazy" became a humorous annotation to a whole new reality for me, which was entrepreneurship. The regular, recurring paycheck of corporate life was replaced by the entrepreneurial style of looking for opportunities, working hard, and curating what success looked like for me.

Sometimes we become so stuck to our stories that we forget we have the power to write them ourselves. We all collect mental clutter on our journey through life. And if we put much weight on it, steering toward our true selves can be difficult. Where might I be, had I let my teachers' comments take hold in my heart? If I had continued to believe that talking too much and having a busy mind are negative qualities?

If we look hard enough, we can find lessons in the oddest places, like in the adjective "lazy."

Some people might call it being still or mindful. Some people might even call it meditation. Call it what you want, but for me, it's lazy.

Being lazy helps us become conscious enough to notice the shoulder taps and to figure out how to use the tools being offered and how to do what we need to, to bring ourselves into alignment. When we notice what values continually pop up in life, the ones that are at play over and over, for us, that's really what living your Everyday Legacy is: discovering what's important to you, putting those values on repeat, and living them every day. Giving them to the people around you, and the world.

CONCLUSION

THE BEGINNING

NOT LONG ago, I was at a retreat with a friend, a fellow professional speaker named Charlotte. We decided to go on a mountain hike together. The view from the top was truly spectacular. We were standing there admiring the beauty around us when Charlotte realized she had a livestream scheduled and she had to check in with her community. She excused herself, and I sat in a red Muskoka chair, taking in the view.

Charlotte was about thirty feet away from me, holding up her phone and chatting with her viewers.

Along came another pair who didn't know that Charlotte and I were together. They started to speak ill of her, loud enough that I could hear them. They said she was being narcissistic, complained that she couldn't put down her phone and just enjoy the view, and griped about other things along those lines.

I had to take several deep breaths to stop myself from approaching them. If they knew Charlotte, they would understand that she's an entirely selfless human being who would bend over backward to do something for anyone. It would break her heart if she heard someone speaking about her the way they spoke.

I wanted to ask them why they would judge her. What if she were recovering from a serious illness and had just hiked up to the top of a mountain and was sending a victory video to her family? Would knowing more about her change their narrative? But I already knew the answer. Of course that would have changed their perspective.

I say all this knowing that I am not perfect.

We may think, *How cruel of those people to judge Charlotte without knowing her circumstances or what she was doing, without knowing anything about her.* But we've all done it. Most of us pass judgment more often than we might like to admit.

Recently, I was out for dinner with a group of friends at a city restaurant. We could see across the street into the windows of a gym, where a man was deadlifting a bar with very little weight on it.

He was making each lift look as if it was taking a considerable amount of effort, one slow rep at a time. I hate to admit it, but my initial reaction was that he looked comical, this man at the gym lifting hardly any weight and struggling so much. But a thought entered my mind that pushed the negativity away: *What if that man had been in a car accident and this was his rehabilitation?* Who was I to judge him for taking the time to go to the gym and move his body again?

Why do we give negativity such a throne to sit on in our minds? I don't know the answer, but I know that too often we are programmed to be more judgmental than gracious.

When we take a moment to consider our thoughts, perhaps in that very instant, we can replace that judgment with a compassionate response and allow ourselves to change the narrative.

When you change your relationship with yourself, you change your relationship with others. When you change your relationship with yourself and others, you see the possibility of humanity. If this book helps you to shift your perspective and make yourself more gracious than judgmental, I consider that a victory. If you are more conscious of how you're showing up and engaging with others in the world, this book has been a success.

We live in a microwave generation. We want everything instantly. The beauty of an Everyday Legacy is that you can implement it right now. There's no secret formula, no gimmick. It's not rocket science. You can start living your Everyday Legacy right now, and the impact will last a lifetime.

All it takes to create positive change is conscious awareness in a world that, for the most part, operates unconsciously. That's the power of realizing your possibility and the possibility in others.

At the beginning of this book, I wrote about Malala Yousafzai. Being shot and nearly killed could have changed the conversation for her to a negative one. She could have accepted a fate of silence and defeat. But she made a different choice. That's what separates people who achieve greatness from those who resolve themselves to a story being written for them as opposed to writing it themselves.

Imagine if you lived more conscious of the influence you have on people's lives. People in a casket at the front of the room don't get to experience this.

But you and me? As long as we still draw breath, we can change how we live. We can't change what's already been written, but we can change our relationship with the words on the page. I can't change what happened with Bob. I could be resolved to the fact that he wasn't a father for me and leave it at that, but I've managed to shift my perspective, which has given me peace.

What's written isn't nearly as important as the most vital chapter—the one being drafted right now. Take a look in the mirror and make sure that person is showing up every day in a way that is purpose- and passion-filled.

Bearing in mind that right now is the most important time in our life, we must find out what truly matters to us and live with those values. Then, not only do we start to change, but we begin to affect the people around us. They start to get what makes us tick, what we're in alignment with, and who we are.

We are in control of our lives. When we begin to grasp the concept of legacy as something that we live rather than something that we leave behind, we change our relationship with ourselves and others. With one tiny shift in perspective, and a new, conscious awareness, the transformation begins.

The end of this book is only the beginning of my Everyday Legacy, and, I hope, the beginning of yours, too.

Rather than merely leaving it behind, may you live your legacy, every single day.

~~The End.~~
The Beginning.

ACKNOWLEDGMENTS

O N A FALL day in September 2017, I began to write this book. It has taken a full year to pull all of these thoughts and ideas together to share with the world. To be honest, I'm struggling with what words I should leave you with. What can I say to you, the reader, that will inspire you to live your Everyday Legacy beyond what I've already said?

Writing this book is part of my own Everyday Legacy, to have an impact on others and affect people in meaningful ways. Writing this book has affected me more than I would ever have imagined.

If the only person who ever reads these words is me, that's okay. If this book never directly changes anyone else's world, that's all right, because the process of writing it changed mine. And I believe that having written it, I won't be able to help but have a more positive impact on others.

This book has changed how I show up every day. It has changed how I engage with myself—my thoughts and behaviors— and how I engage with others.

Writing about my relationship with Bob has given me even more closure and clarity around that complicated part of my life, which I now understand was one of the most beautiful relationships I have ever had, even in its state of disrepair.

Writing this book has deepened my understanding of ego and how everything comes down to perspective.

This year of reflection has strengthened my connection to the Universe, helping me to pay even more attention to the many shoulder taps that continue to come my way.

Writing this book has helped me to connect with finger snap people who will be part of my life forever. It has helped me to have more empathy for my fellow human beings.

It has made me a better man.

To say that I did this alone would be a grand fabrication.

I've always admired people's greatness—their expertise— and loved meeting people who are recognized for their craft:

Jaime Lee Mann, whose coaching and mentorship in a space I knew so little about—book writing—helped shape my thoughts and develop my ideas.

Page Two—my publisher—and my entire team there, who made my dream of publishing a book come true, with grace, finesse, and loving compassion at every turn.

Kendra Ward—my editor—who became a kindred spirit as we navigated taking my manuscript from where it was to the book you hold now, and who did so with love and precision.

John Sweet—my copy editor—whose skill at refining the English language and whose way with words elevated this book to new heights.

And finally, those whom I consider experts at love and support, Eric and my family:

Eric—whose patience and unrelenting support, I dare to say, is like nothing I've ever experienced, and which I'm grateful for every single day.

My mother—Sandi—who has been my number one fan and cheerleader; whom I can always count on, no matter what. Her endless love and encouragement is fuel to my already ambitious fire.

And finally, to my family—whose roots I'm so proud to share.

I love you all, so much.

ABOUT THE AUTHOR

"A LEGACY IS something you live, not what you leave behind." So believes Codi Shewan, who spent two decades working in the death-care profession, until in 2014 he leapt from an executive position in corporate funeral services to the entrepreneurial world. As a consultant and speaker, he's on a mission to redefine "legacy" as something that you personify, each day of your life: you can realize the power of your own positive influence while you're still here. He is also the founder of From Strangers To Family, an experience which helps people feel connected, in an often disconnected world.

www.everydaylegacy.com